continued

Language and Literacy Series, *continued*

Curating a Literacy Life

Student-Centered Learning With Digital Media

William Kist

With Shannon Davis and Ga-Vita Haynes

Foreword by Ernest Morrell

TEACHERS COLLEGE PRESS

TEACHERS COLLEGE | COLUMBIA UNIVERSITY
NEW YORK AND LONDON

Published by Teachers College Press,® 1234 Amsterdam Avenue, New York, NY 10027

Front cover design by Peter Donahue. Image by Davide Angelini / Adobe Stock.

Library of Congress Cataloging-in-Publication Data is available at loc.gov

ISBN 978-0-8077-6658-3 (paper)
ISBN 978-0-8077-6659-0 (hardcover)
ISBN 978-0-8077-8084-8 (ebook)

Printed on acid-free paper
Manufactured in the United States of America

Contents

Joyful Learning, Reading, and Writing the World in the Digital Age

Education Week recently ran a story about the "real reasons kids aren't reading anymore," citing YouTube, TikTok, and other video-sharing sites as the culprits (Klein, 2022). An often-cited 2019 survey conducted by Common Sense Media found that kids and teens spend between 5 to 7 and a half hours a day on social media (Rideout & Robb, 2019). If we rely on a narrow definition of "reading," particularly of traditional print and texts limited primarily to novels, these findings could lead us to believe that children and young people's literacy skills and ability to read the word and the world (Freire, 1970) is diminishing—and that social media is to blame. The children and young people referred to in these articles and surveys have only known a world in which technology, screens, and the internet are ubiquitous. Social and digital media are not going away. Rather than wishing an unrealistic return to a world dominated by traditional print technology, it is far more productive to help young people become critical consumers, producers, and curators of media if we want to develop joyful, engaged, and reflective learners who are able to read and write the world in the digital age.

Based on his work with English teachers and students at a high school in Cleveland that began in 2018, William Kist offers a four-part process to help young people "curate" (Collect, Organize, Repurpose, and Reflect) digital work and various texts in purposeful and intentional ways. He weaves in the rich and authentic voices of English teachers who offer invaluable insights for understanding the school culture, students, and community as well as their innovative approaches to using curation and technology to teach new and traditional texts. What began with a contract from the Institute for Student Achievement to serve as an instructional coach, visiting the school weekly to work with English teachers, led to reading books, publishing a journal article, presenting at state and national conferences *together*, and, ultimately, the creation of this book.

Rather than punishing students or eliminating students' use of their cellphones in class, teachers encouraged students to use their hand-held computers as invaluable resources to research various topics and engage in project-based learning via culturally relevant pedagogy (Ladson-Billings, 1995). When we quickly moved to online learning in the midst of the pandemic in March 2020, Kist observed teachers innovatively pairing popular novels such as *The Hate U Give* with the "classic" *Antigone* and incorporating various "new literacies" and multimodalities—effectively blurring the line between in-school and out-of-school literacies for young people. Students were well prepared to use basic technology, such as smartphones, when they were physically outside of school to continue to engage in meaningful academic work.

Kist argues that the traditional literacy pedagogy he continues to see in classrooms lacks meaningful and engaged reading and writing. He juxtaposes "sleepy lessons" in schools with the amount of reading and writing happening in coffee shops with "good Wi-Fi" and wonders how we generate this same type of engagement, "flow," and energy in classrooms (p. 11, this volume). We see the lingering and residual impact of the pandemic in education as traditional models of schooling lead us to rightly question how we teach young people to read and write. Kist challenges readers to consider how new literacies can serve as a boon to old literacies where intertextuality and allusions to a variety of texts can lead to rich conversations, engagement, and joy.

Finally, Kist sums up the English teachers' practices as encompassing a "funds-of-knowledge, inquiry-driven, digital-media-and-arts–inclusive teaching philosophy" (p. 14) by helping students to become curators of various texts using screen-based devices and encouraging them to draw on their everyday experiences. He asserts that remote learning has had a significant impact on pedagogical approaches and the projects and assignments he describes in his book, regardless of setting (at home or in a brick-and-mortar school). The majority of his timely and accessible book details each aspect of the four-part process of becoming curators and offers concrete examples by English teachers, packed with various strategies and assessments.

William Kist has thoroughly and respectfully documented the innovative work of English teachers who value and enact culturally responsive pedagogy with project-based learning, inquiry-based lessons, meaningful use of technology, and multimodalities. Drawing on theories of social justice pedagogy and critical media pedagogy, Kist's four-part model of curation is less of a formula than a model for a student-centered approach that can be adapted to any learning environment. It's easy to tell educators to acknowledge the role social media and technology play in the lives of our young people; it's quite another endeavor to provide a flexible model applicable across various spaces with concrete examples of what bringing this theory to practice looks like with teachers and students.

—Ernest Morrell, University of Notre Dame

REFERENCES

Freire, P. (1970). *Pedagogy of the oppressed*. Continuum.

Klein, A. (2022, March 28). The real reasons kids aren't reading more. *Education Week*. https://www.edweek.org/leadership/the-real-reasons-kids-arent-reading-more/2022/03

Ladson-Billings, G. (1995). Toward a theory of culturally relevant pedagogy. *American Educational Research Journal*, 32(3), 465–491. https://doi.org/10.3102/00028312032003465

Rideout, V., & Robb, M. (2019, October 28). *The Common Sense census: Media use by tweens and teens, 2019*. https://www.commonsensemedia.org/sites/default/files/research/report/2019-census-8-to-18-full-report-updated.pdf

Acknowledgments

This book would not have happened if I had not gotten the job as instructional coach at Glenville High School. So, of course I need to acknowledge my colleagues from both the Institute of Student Achievement (ISA) and The National Center for Restructuring Education (NCREST)—Betty Greene-Bryant, senior director of programs at ISA, and director of NCREST Janet Price. I must single out Sylvia Rabiner, from NCREST, who read my logs each month and always provided such sound and supportive feedback. I must also credit the now-retired director of NCREST, Jackie Ancess, who was the one who hired me for this work before she retired. Finally, I must acknowledge the president of ISA, Stephanie Wood-Garnett, a Cleveland native! Stephanie has been unfailingly positive and supportive of our work at Glenville and of this book. To her credit, all she has asked for is a copy (autographed) of the book once it's published.

I want to thank the person who had the original connection to ISA and who brought the organization to Glenville, Sam Scavella. Thank you, Sam! And, of course, there would be no book if it were not for Jacqueline Bell, who has been principal of Glenville since 1999. I also want to acknowledge Lavora "Gayle" Gadison, social studies content manager for the Cleveland Metropolitan School District. Gayle was the link between Glenville and Paul Sapin, the documentary filmmaker whose work is described in Chapter 4.

Above all, I want to give a shout out to the teachers with whom I met on a weekly basis beginning in 2018, including not only Shannon Davis and Ga-Vita Haynes, who contributed to this book, but also Shanita Horton, Elaine Griffin, Christopher Serio, Andretta Montgomery, Kimberly Golphin, Louie Moore, Amy Furmanek, Keisha Davenport, Yvonne Renee Wright, and Robyn Williamson.

And the Glenville students! What can I say about them? Their courage on a daily basis humbles me.

It has been great to return to Teachers College Press, and I must give a shout out to Carol Chambers Collins, who gave me my first break back in 2004 and edited my first book for TCP, *New Literacies in Action*. Over the years, I've kept in touch with TCP and have ended up having a great experience working with my current editor, Emily Spangler. Her intelligence, wisdom, and patience have been wonderful assets for this project, which has spanned a pandemic, racial and political struggles and, as I write this, the beginning of a war in Europe. I'll always be appreciative that Emily met with me, Shannon Davis, Ga-Vita Haynes, and Shanita Horton at the National Council of Teachers of English Annual Convention in Baltimore in November, 2019. Emily was gently supportive and guided us through the process of preparing the book proposal. I also want to give a shout out to TCP production editor John Bylander and copy editor Nancy Mandel, who provided extremely close readings and precise comments. Any errors or omissions that are still evident are, ultimately, my mistakes, not theirs.

And what an honor that Ernest Morrell has written the foreword to this book! I have known Ernest for about 20 years, through our work together on projects for the National Council of Teachers of English. Thank you, Ernest!

During the writing of the book, I was able to rely on my own copy editor and assistant, Sharon Smith, who has helped me with so many projects over the years, including the digitizing of many of my files. Regarding digitizing, I must also give a shout out to my assistants at Kent State University, Sherry Ernsberger and Katherine Bryk. All three—Sharon, Sherry, and Katherine—helped me digitize a couple decades' worth of files so that I was ready to write this book when it was time to do so.

On the home front, I am blessed to be married to the amazing Stephanie Kandel Kist, who is not only my wonderful wife and life partner, but also a superb writer and editor in her own right. Not only did she give the manuscript a read and provide welcome comments, she also supplied the strong support and encouragement that only she can bring. And, of course, our children—Mariel, Liam, and Vivienne—give me inspiration every day as they go about curating their digital lives.

Finally, I want to make sure to mention with pride that I come from a family of teachers. I've thought of the teachers in my family often as I've written this book. As I write this, my mother, Dorothy Levering Kist, is weeks away from turning 90. She is a former 2nd-grade teacher at Seiberling Elementary in the Akron Public Schools. I've thought a lot about her as I've been writing this book. She is the one who told me when I was a child that I couldn't have a birthday party unless we invited my entire class. And so we did invite the entire class, every year, all 32 of them. I like to think my mother's spirit of righteous inclusiveness is present throughout this book. My mother's parents, Treva and Miles Levering, were also teachers. The taught during the 1920s at London High School, in London, Ohio. Treva's mother, Sophie Holt Locke, while not a teacher, came from a family that ran what was called a "normal" school in the mid-1800s—a school for people who wanted to be teachers. Sophie was born in 1876 and lived until 1977. I have fond memories of her as well as of my mother's brother, Richard Levering, who was a high school English teacher at Garfield High School in the Akron Public Schools. My uncle, after a career in the military, taught high school English until he was 76 years old. I've felt their presence during the writing of this book, as well as the presence of my dad's mother, Dorothy Keller. She read aloud to my brother, sister, and me religiously and was a teacher in her own way, as she worked her magic in the kitchen for each of our holidays and introduced us to the Peanuts comic strip. I've thought of my own family quite often as I've been writing this book, because of the family feeling that permeates Glenville. Ms. Bell and the teachers at Glenville have welcomed me into their family. I have felt loved, and I have loved them. This book is dedicated to them.

Introduction

Each of us is a curator—a selector, an evaluator, an organizer, a displayer—of the many texts we encounter in our works and lives. As we download personal photos from our phones, organize our playlists on Spotify, and chronicle our experiences and feelings on social media, we are, essentially, curating our literacy lives. What if we were more purposeful and intentional about this process, more conscious of how we make use of texts, from the ones we collect and organize to the ones we repurpose and reflect on? This book sets forth a four-step process to help kids manage and even thrive in the midst of the deluge of media messages that has come to be a part of our everyday lives. I borrow a term from the art world and call this *curation*.

In the context of Glenville High School in Cleveland, Ohio, I tinkered with a model I had been developing over several years based on the curation concept. In weekly meetings with the Glenville English teachers, we discussed the applicability of the curation model, but mostly we discussed the challenges of teaching English at the high school level in a new media age; we read books together; we wrote together; we told stories. This book came out of these discussions.

I first became interested in using *curation* as a way of thinking about new literacies (i.e., the literacies that have developed around multimedia and digital texts) based on my own collecting of texts, which has been somewhat compulsive over the years. I think many teachers are pack rats, and I qualify. I collect texts (books, films, pieces of art) because of my own enjoyment of them, but I also always have my "teacher hat" on, thinking how I can use a text in some future lesson or unit. As we have moved into the digital age, collecting texts has fortunately become more manageable, and I have found myself digitizing many texts I have collected over the years. My home office is still somewhat of a candidate for an episode of *Hoarders*, but digitizing my various files and texts has led to a greater level of efficiency in using my collection, an efficiency that has benefited me and, I hope, benefited my students. As I have moved into parenthood, I have been amazed at how many times I have been able to pull out a text or even an object that can make for a "teachable moment" or just a pleasurable exchange with my own children. If I hadn't been intentional about curating my literacy life, organizing it in a comprehendible and accessible way, I would have missed some meaningful moments with my children, my students, and the teachers with whom I work at Glenville.

This book is an end product of the curating that I've done—in this case collecting, organizing, and repurposing a collection of assignments and assessments related to the concept of curation itself. Contained herein are many assignments and activities that I've developed over the years as well as contributions from two of the Glenville teachers with whom I worked, Shannon Davis and Ga-Vita Haynes. These are exercises and prompts that can help any teacher, not only English teachers. I believe many of these strategies can also be useful for parents and students on the home front.

At Glenville, it seemed like using curation as an overarching way of thinking about literacies helped me give some structure and meaning to what I was witnessing. And what I was seeing was a dissolution of the divide between school-based and home-based literacies, a divide that seems to have always challenged educators. I was also seeing great examples of culturally responsive teaching. As I heard the conversations around various texts in the classrooms, I began to have difficulty differentiating Glenville the school from Glenville the community. I got to see how students encountered a range of texts from so-called "high art" to so-called "low art," and the artificiality and contrivance of traditional school seemed to be even more evident than it typically is. I was witnessing students curating their literacy lives. This book portrays how this can take place, really, in any school, and be extended outside of school.

Starting with *Collecting* and followed up by *Organizing*, *Repurposing*, and *Reflecting*, this *Curation Model* comprises the recursive nature of capturing, making meaning, and then creating our own representations of ourselves and of the world. This book provides real-world examples of how thinking about these steps has been helpful in one high school, complete with a variety of assignments and activities from the simple to the complex. If you work with kids or you live with kids, this book should help you harness the potential that exists as we all try to navigate the texts that constantly surround us.

ORIGINS OF THIS BOOK

The conversation at Glenville High School that led to this book began in the fall of 2018 and hasn't stopped. I accepted a contract from the Institute for Student Achievement to be an instructional coach, working with English teachers, and I've been visiting Glenville (either in person or virtually) every week since then. I was pleased to be asked to work for The Institute for Student Achievement (https://www.studentachievement.org/), which is partnered with the National Center for Restructuring Education, Schools and Teaching (https://www.tc.columbia.edu/ncrest/), because I felt in sync with their principles and mission. Quoting from their website: "For nearly 30 years, the Institute for Student Achievement (ISA) has partnered with schools and districts to transform schools so that students who are traditionally underserved and underperforming graduate prepared for success in college and careers" (Institute for Student Achievement, 2021). The organization emphasizes a student-driven inquiry approach to curriculum and instruction.

Glenville High School has a rich past (and present). Located in the neighborhood of Glenville in Cleveland, the school has graduated such disparate luminaries as media mogul Lew Wasserman; film producer Ross Hunter; television celebrity Steve Harvey; Joe Shuster and Jerry Siegel (the two men who created Superman); and about 20 current and former NFL players. During the early part of the 20th century, Glenville was a predominantly Jewish neighborhood within the city of Cleveland. Another famous alumna from this earlier era is noted literacy researcher Yetta Goodman.

After World War II, the neighborhood changed and became predominantly African American. The school became a frequent stop for politicians and icons such as Martin Luther King Jr., who gave a speech at the school on April 26, 1967 (https://www.youtube.com/watch?v=IMMxhjFYBgM). One of the quotes from his speech that day is writ large on the wall of the cafeteria: "I urge you today to realize that doors of opportunities are opening now that were not open to our mothers and our fathers. And the great challenge facing each of you today is to be ready to enter these doors as they open."

The Glenville neighborhood is also famous for the violence, referred to as the "Glenville shoot-out," that occurred there in July of 1968. There has been much controversy over what happened during that tumultuous week in which three police officers and three members of the radical group Black Nationalists of New Libya were killed. Some say that the neighborhood has never recovered from what happened during that week in 1968. As I started work at the school in 2018, little did I know that the students and teachers had been wrapped up in making a video documentary, under the guidance of an award-winning documentarian, about these events and their implications for the current young people of Glenville. More about that project in a later chapter.

As Ga-Vita Haynes, one of the Glenville English teachers, describes Glenville: "I see a building that is family oriented and that gives students opportunities to grow and prosper. In addition, I see students who want to learn in a safe environment. I hear intelligent educators who teach students how to learn and use their voices to change the issues seen in their community. I hear scared voices that realize they can become whoever they want if they believe in themselves. But they need adults to reassure that they are someone who can change the world." All of these elements were clearly in evidence in the fall of 2018 when I started visiting Glenville. As Mrs. Haynes points out, there were longstanding elders in the community who had been those reassuring voices. "People who graduated years ago, in the 70s and 80s, come back and contribute to different scholarships. When we have book fairs at the local Barnes and Noble, the Glenville community supports the students through their contributions. . . . Glenville families truly depend on the community and staff to protect their students when they send them to school. Glenville is built on strength, loyalty, and dedication." And Glenville has been making progress academically. For the last three years, the school has earned a "Momentum" award from the Ohio Department of Education because they have shown and exceeded student growth on three metrics: Schools must earn straight As on all value-added measures on the state "report card," which is the term used in Ohio for an evaluation of each school provided to the general public. And the school must have at least two value-added subgroups of students, which includes gifted, lowest 20% in achievement, and students with disabilities (Ohio Department of Education, 2020).

I remember driving into the Glenville neighborhood for the first time. It seemed like a typical urban neighborhood, with some homes well-kept and some not. I drove by a corner market called the Red Apple Supermarket that could have been Maverick Carter's grocery store in *The Hate U Give* (Thomas, 2017), complete with a cacophony of signs and advertisements and a gate pulled over the door. I also drove by churches, a beautiful public library branch, and various fast-food restaurants. When I drove up to the school, it looked like a typical huge brick school building dating to the 1960s. A playground fence enclosed the parking lot. I walked in alongside students who were oblivious to anything but getting where they were going. I began visiting the classrooms of the English teachers that morning and was welcomed immediately. I had been hired to go to Glenville once a week to help the English teachers. But I soon found out that they didn't need much help from me. They just needed an outside pair of eyes, someone to reflect back, someone to riff with, as we began to do during our weekly conversations.

A lot of what I did involved listening. I listened to the teachers' stories. Ga-Vita Haynes had been a teacher in the Glenville neighborhood schools since 2001 when I met her in 2018. She writes, "As I reflect on my years at Glenville High School, the school culture has changed over time. When I moved from the elementary level to Glenville High in 2010, I was anxious to see how high school students learn and I wanted to grasp their attitude towards their educational career paths and their personal lives, and understand where they see themselves when they graduate from high school. Building relationships with students and their families was the number one goal I wanted to accomplish my first year teaching high school. My first year, I taught English to 11th- and 12th-grade students. Mind you, this was my first year ever teaching teenagers—prior years, I taught 3rd- and 5th-graders at an elementary school for nine years. I did not have a clue what to expect from high school young adults. My first day, I was stern, and my students understood the goals I wanted them to accomplish by the end of the school year. But standardized testing sometimes gets in the way of a teacher's creativity. More than ever, I had many questions about why students need to pass seven different Ohio Graduation Tests to receive a diploma. Most students were not going to attend college but needed basic skills in order to survive and sustain a job. I started teaching 'nontraditional' lessons because I knew my students needed these skills after graduation. Sometimes, I was called on it, for an explanation as to why I was not teaching to the test. I wanted to show the administration that teaching to the test will not help my students survive after graduation—they needed more than test skills. They needed more skills including typing, resume writing, cooking, and communicating via the growing technology.

"My teaching began at Empire Computech Elementary, in the Glenville neighborhood, in 2001. I enjoyed my career there for nine years. Beginning my teaching career in elementary prepared me for the position I have today. Many experiences helped me understand the educational system and how students need more than just the textbook we present to them for knowledge. They need exposure to the world. So, for four years, towards the end of my career at Empire Computech, I began to take my students on field trips to Washington DC. During those four trips, one of the adventures was to listen to the first Black president ever elected in the United States, Barack Obama. What an experience! During those days, the students were eager to come to class and complete assignments.

"Making the transition to teaching at the high school level was challenging, but those first students I had to this day call me to get advice about life decisions. I wanted to have relationships that last for a lifetime, so that my students are able to keep in touch to let me know how they are doing in their personal lives or ask me for some advice. We had an opportunity to develop an afterschool program for the students. We thought it would be difficult for students to want to participate if we were not offering food or money. So, we offered snacks and food for the students to stay after school for tutoring or field trip experiences.

"This past year and a half has been challenging for teachers and students. We were all trying to figure out ways to service students and give them the best education career during the pandemic while teaching and learning remotely. I had the opportunity last school year to set up a Zoom appearance by Glenville alumni Steve Harvey. He was able to speak to some of our graduates from Glenville High School. They were very pleased with the surprise guest that day, and he encouraged them to be the best they can be from where they are coming from. In addition, he told them they can do whatever they want to do in this life. The Zoom meeting was uplifting and convinced the students to want more out of life after they graduate from high school."

I listened to stories such as these from Mrs. Haynes, and the other Glenville English teachers, and I told them my own story as a classroom teacher in an urban school who defined "reading" and "writing" broadly. During our weekly meetings, we kind of riffed on our various experiences, both recent and far in the past. We would talk about assignments that had worked and assignments that didn't work. We talked about a variety of texts—books, films, television shows, songs. We ended up reading several books together. I took notes on our conversations, typing them out on a laptop as we talked. I mainly did this so that I could remember the things they said, including what help they needed from me. I soon began to feel that we had a story to tell. In 2019, I suggested that we might want to document our work, and this led to a presentation at our state affiliate of the National Council of Teachers of English (called the Ohio Council of Teachers of English), and an article for our state journal (Kist et al., 2019). This led, eventually, to a presentation at the National Council of Teachers of English in Baltimore, in November 2019, where we met Emily Spangler, acquisitions editor from Teachers College Press. All of this led up to the book you are now reading. Two of the Glenville teachers—Shannon Davis and Ga-Vita Haynes—agreed to contribute to this book in the form of providing assignments and descriptions of their work. Our conversations all along have focused on the innovative ways that the Glenville teachers have been reaching out to their students and on innovative ideas we would like to try, and how the curation model could be useful for organizing our ideas.

The very first spark of this book came from a lesson I observed in Shannon Davis's sophomore English class in the fall of 2018. Ms. Davis was discussing a section of the book *The Hate U Give* (Thomas, 2017) with the focus being student voice. The guiding question was: How did the central character, Starr Carter, give voice to the injustices she was seeing around her? (The book's plot centers on Starr's attempt to cope with witnessing a police shooting of a boy she was riding in a car with.)

After guiding students to find textual evidence of Starr's speaking out in the novel, Ms. Davis directed students to take out their phones. This definitely got my attention, because I'm so used to being in schools in which phones are forbidden in classrooms. The students were to research a list of athletes who have raised their voices in the past. Ms. Davis provided several examples, including Colin Kaepernick, Muhammad Ali, Serena Williams, and, from the 1968 Summer Olympics, Tommie Smith and John Carlos. But students were also welcome to find their own examples. Before I knew it, students were in small groups reading about these real-life activists on their phones. Ultimately, the students were to respond to a few prompts that asked them to write about what social injustice was being protested by the athlete and why the issue was important to that athlete at that time in history.

Not only was I impressed that Ms. Davis was allowing students to use their phones, I was also impressed by how engaged the students were, how socially relevant the topic was, and the ease with which Ms. Davis moved back and forth between traditional and new media. I felt that she was modeling for students how they might use their devices "in real life," looking up some facts about a topic or issue that they were interested in. I thought that this lesson was meaningful on several levels. She was, of course, helping kids see the relevance of the book they were reading, perhaps motivating them to keep reading. But she was also demonstrating a way of collecting, organizing, and repurposing, in that they were expected to find examples of speaking out and then repurposing these examples into a new text of their own.

I would routinely see Ms. Davis take something from her anthology and riff on it. For instance, recently, before reading a *New York Times* editorial about the 1994 caning of 18-year-old Michael Fay in Singapore ("Time To Assert American Values," 1994), Ms. Davis played a YouTube clip she found about Kim Kardashian's intervention to obtain a pardon for Alice Johnson, a 63-year-old grandmother serving a life sentence. (Michael Fay was a youth who was punished in 1994 for vandalizing cars in Singapore. Alice Johnson had been in prison since 1996 for drug trafficking until Kim Kardashian got involved with her case.) The op-ed about mistreatment of an American in Singapore almost 30 years ago came alive for students as they formed a mini-text set related to the issue of crime and punishment. I would routinely see Ms. Davis and the other teachers at Glenville make these kinds of connections, taking remote material and making it current and, often, multimodal.

Ms. Davis was making use of the available "new literacies" and exemplifying culturally responsive teaching as I understand it (Gay, 2018; Ladson-Billings, 2014). Gay (2018) admits that many of the terms currently in use (she lists culturally relevant, culturally responsive, sensitive, centered, congruent, reflective, mediated, contextualized, synchronized, and responsive) are, essentially, describing the same concept—"the ideas about why it is important to make classroom instruction more consistent with the cultural orientations of ethnically diverse students, and how this can be done, are virtually identical" (p. 36). Ms. Davis and her colleagues were creating affirming classrooms; they weren't looking at their students with a deficit perspective. And I saw most students rise to the occasion.

One of my weekly practices with the ELA faculty at Glenville was to facilitate a meeting during common planning time so that we could debrief about what we had been experiencing in the classrooms. In our conversations, I highlighted the seamless way that Ms. Davis and others were using various media texts and devices, weaving together canonical pieces of literature with pop culture and current events. They were helping their students experience how their daily literacy practices had value both inside and outside of school.

And I increasingly came to believe that the various strategies I was seeing fell into a model I had been playing with for several years, a model based on my impression of what a museum curator does (Kist, 2019). I was seeing similarities to many of the "new literacies" instructional strategies that I'd been collecting over the years (Kist, 2005, 2010, 2013). At Glenville, students (and the teachers themselves) would read and view various texts ("collecting" them), and then they would organize them, present them, and repurpose them in new ways. There would also be some kind of reflection, an assessment of what had been learned and of the experience itself. I saw the process of curating as comprising both very individual acts and very collaborative, public acts—each learner attempts to curate a literacy life and to make sense of the world in a recursive, ongoing way. Meeting with the teachers on a weekly basis stimulated me to go back through many of the favorite assignments I have either developed myself or collected, forming a kind of review of my own curating on this topic.

MAKING MY OWN CONNECTIONS

As I watched the kids at Glenville, I thought not only of many of my former students but also my own children. In 2012, my wife, Stephanie, and I became parents in a very big way. We welcomed our triplets—Mariel, Liam, and Vivienne—into the world. As I worked at Glenville, I also was thinking about curation as I watched my own children, who seemed intent on collecting, organizing, repurposing, and reflecting their own favorite texts and objects from a very early age. Over the years, I had brought out some of my own old toys and books for them and revisited some objects and texts that I had collected and organized for years; I was impelled to think about the way I keep, organize, and repurpose those important items in my own life.

This rumination on the idea of curation was refined and further stimulated by the major world events of 2020—the ongoing spotlight on racial injustice and the world pandemic. My weekly conversations with the Glenville teachers went virtual, as did their instruction. I also became much more heavily involved in the education of my own children, who were summarily sent home, as was the entire world, in March 2020. In my own life, I was seeing a blurring of out-of-school and in-school literacies. I would reflect back to the teachers some of the strategies I was using with my children, as the Glenville teachers told me about the challenges of moving online. This, in turn, would prompt me to bring material from my files related to the new literacies teaching that I had witnessed over my years of work. What I saw the Glenville teachers doing was, again, riffing, letting one idea or text ricochet into another, however unexpected—pairing *The Hate U Give* with *Antigone*, for instance—to catch students' interest and ignite new ideas. This made me think about what I was doing years ago in my own classroom without realizing what I was doing. I remembered that what had started me down this road was joy and happiness. I felt joy experiencing certain texts in my own life; I felt joy sharing these texts with my students; and now I was experiencing joy sharing texts with my own children as they shared some of their favorite texts with me.

Back toward the beginning of my career, I started researching new literacies in classrooms because I had success using video in my own classroom back in the 1990s, just as the Internet was beginning to infiltrate our lives. I discovered this passion for multimodality from several experiences I had with my students, including the day that I showed them a very old media text, a silent film, Charles Chaplin's *The Kid* (Chaplin, 1921). I looked around the room as they stared at the screen, practically immobilized with the story of the tramp's attempt to adopt an orphan. I had been inspired by an offhand comment in the teacher's manual of my course textbook, an anthology of canonical literature, of all things. The comment suggested, very briefly, that teachers should consider teaching a unit in film literacy. I had access to some old films, and started showing them, beginning with *The Kid*. Before long, we were using these films (as well as canonical texts) to discuss all kinds of media and how storytellers use these media to communicate. This was a natural fit for me as I had grown up from a very young age loving all sorts of film and television, in addition to comic books, music and, of course, books. I had begged my parents (successfully) to allow me to stay up very late, in 1972, to see Chaplin accept his honorary Oscar. My sister, Nancy, and I used to act out Chaplin scenes for my grandmother, Treva Locke Levering, who was born in 1898 and remembered seeing Chaplin films as they were released in the 1910s and 1920s.

I found that my 9th-grade English classroom became an extension of myself. I created an enriched learning community that included film and video. My students not only watched Charlie and The Kid, they soon also became busy making parodies of commercials and producing their own MTV videos. I found an unused piano in my school and asked my principal, Mr. Raoul Bolock, if it could be moved to my classroom. Even though I was an English teacher, he agreed. (Thank you, Mr. Bolock!) I would play the piano for the students as they wrote or as they read. I showed films, I showed TV shows, the students acted out Shakespeare. I like to think that my classroom was a kind of salon, a place in which all kinds of forms of representation were on an equal basis. And this was before we talked about "new literacies" or "multiliteracies" or "multimodalities."

I felt that I was onto something as a classroom teacher and went on to formally research these ideas as I found, through "snowball sampling"

(Merriam, 1998), six classrooms in which teachers were embracing various media. I based my first book on this research, and it was published in 2005 (Kist, 2005). Being in the classrooms I profiled was an exhilarating experience. But it didn't take long for me to realize that these vibrant learning spaces were not being sustained either schoolwide (within the buildings where I was observing these teachers) or across the field of English teaching as a whole. They tended to be isolated examples of new literacies, similar to the way that my experience showing silent movies and playing the piano for my students was a solitary experience in the school where I was teaching.

Over at least the last 20 years, there has been continuing interest in how we can make school more relevant, how we can unite the out-of-school and in-school literacies of our young people, especially for those who live in urban settings (Moje, 2008; Kinloch et al., 2017; Street, 2012), but that interest often does not seem to translate into daily classroom practices across classrooms within a school or, certainly, a district. And yet I continue to be amazed at the depth of intertextual knowledge students have about pop culture—everything from detailed memories of every episode of *SpongeBob SquarePants* to the nuances of the different houses of Hogwarts. I will often be in a classroom observing a teacher trying to get "control" of a runaway conversation about some movie or TV show, trying to drive the conversation back to whatever canonical text is supposed to be the focus. As I watch this scene, I will wonder why the teacher is trying to get the conversation back "on task." Why aren't more teachers making use of the extensive storytelling heritage of these pop culture texts, either by assigning students to compile text sets or just taking a few moments to reference pop culture texts during a classroom discussion? Why not let kids talk about the labyrinthine plotting of the *Star Wars* or Marvel films and their ancillary products? And would it hurt teachers to maybe put up some posters of current films, television programs, and musicians?

Unfortunately, as I get into schools, I'm seeing the same kinds of lessons that I could have seen in 1975. Students are expected to read X number of chapters in a book that the entire class is reading together. For homework, they answer some questions that lead to a test that probably includes some multiple-choice questions and maybe a few extended-response questions, similar in format, perhaps, to whatever the statewide standardized test is. I see students being asked occasionally to write a longer-form literary criticism paper. Often the most involved writing assignment I see is the classic research paper assignment.

And the predominant in-class activity I'm seeing is round-robin reading aloud, sometimes of an entire novel. Or the teacher plays an audiobook version of the novel as the students read along. My own anecdotal observations are backed up by years of research that have shown the lack of meaningful reading and writing taking place in our schools. For decades, much of what has happened in English/language arts courses has consisted of almost a cat-echism of call and response, with an emphasis on fact-level questioning (Res-nick, 1991). Students do amazingly little reading and writing on a daily basis (Applebee & Langer, 2011); they are not asked to make meaningful connec-tions linking what they read with their lives as advocated by Rosenblatt's reader response theory, which dates to the 1930s (Rosenblatt, 1938/1955).

At the same time these sleepy lessons are taking place in our schools, walk into any coffee shop that has good Wi-Fi and there will be much more reading and writing and talking going on (with coffee shop customers busy curating their own learning) than in our literacy classrooms. In these dens of java consumption, there is a hum of activity that practically drowns out the smooth jazz that is piped into the background. The customers seem to line up not only for their nonfat caramel macchiatos, but for the "flow" state that working in a coffee house seems to engender. A recent *New Yorker* cartoon built on this idea as a coffee patron looks over at another customer who is deeply engrossed in his laptop and asks him, "I'm sorry to bother you, but I was wondering if I could borrow a little work?"

What is going on in these coffee houses that inspires people to sit for hours reading and writing, perhaps only getting up once for a refill? And why does a coffee shop seem like more of a hotbed of literacy than a typical high school classroom? What's wrong with this picture? What could we do to help make our schools have that same hum of literacy activity?

This book was written during 2020 and 2021, as we have been experi-encing (at least) two major historic events that might finally push us to break out of our humdrum literacy instructional model. In a post-virus world, it's clear that we still need school in some form, but what will school look like now that we've gone through this trial run with remote learning? And what will school look like once we get on the other side of the uncivil "debate" we are having about whether our schools are systemically racist? There is an interesting collision of controversies here, as the pandemic has made many realize how little they miss those biased standardized tests. Seemingly few complained, in the spring of 2020, when most standardized tests were sum-marily canceled by states across the country. In a post-pandemic world, will we take this opportunity to make some substantial changes to the way we do school not only in terms of assessment but also in terms of equity? Or will we just go back to the same old, same old?

The bottom line is that we have, for many years, tolerated a system that is increasingly irrelevant to students' lives outside of school. It's a sys-tem that is unfair to many students from kindergarten on. Some students learn how to play the game of school from an early age, almost as they would learn a ritual, and these students prosper (McLaren, 1986/1999). Many other students don't prosper, and we end up with some 40 percent of incoming high-schoolers needing some kind of remediation. The joke might very well be, however, on those who know how to play the "school" game, as they graduate into a world that might not prize that 4-year bachelor's degree as much as it used to. Even some of the licensed professions, such as medicine and law, are rethinking the way they train their initiates so that emphasis is given to a broader skillset than is represented by grade-point averages. Increasingly, colleges and universities are even beginning to look beyond ACT and SAT scores as they decide upon whom to admit.

The good news is that our schools have a much greater potential for differentiation and fairness than at any other time in history. We have had glimpses of this nirvana for years, from the arts-in-education scholars who made their points before screens came to dominate our literacies, that allowing students a broader palette can help even basic reading comprehension, not to mention student engagement (Eisner, 1997, 2002, 2005; Greene, 2001). And we've been warned for years that the autonomous view of literacy shuts down marginalized youth (Delpit, 1995; Delpit and Dowdy, 2008; Freire, 1970; Morrell et al., 2013).

A silver lining of the pandemic is that it has revealed these early proponents of multimodality as prophetic. Being able to read and write critically and authentically in a screen-based environment has never been so valuable. Whether we like it or not, it is difficult to think of any task in this "gig economy" in which a person will not need to be able to read and write efficiently and deeply via a screen. And regardless of the occupational necessities of navigating different kinds of texts, it's clear that our students (for the most part) are leading wired lives as part of their pursuit of happiness. The Pew Internet and American Life Project continues to provide documentation of the prevalence of screens in the lives of young people, specifically in the form of smartphones. According to a 2021 report from the Pew Research Center on mobile technology and home broadband use, smartphone ownership continues to grow among American adults (to 85%). Some 91% of adults report either having a smartphone or a broadband subscription. Interestingly, about 28% of adults ages 18 to 29 are in the "smartphone-only" category of internet users (Perrin, 2021).

The reality is that a large number of young people are accessing the internet only via their phones. An irony of this disconnect between our schools and the outside world is that phones continue to be banned in some schools, at least within the classroom. I was shocked into realizing the usual disconnect between school-based and out-of-school-based literacies when I heard Ms. Davis at Glenville so casually say, "Everyone take out your phones. I want you to look something up for me." Great! Why not? Isn't that what we all do outside of school?

The teachers I worked with at Glenville didn't seem to have any hang-ups about pop culture. They had bigger fish to fry. They got past any biases they had about screen-based media and realized that it allowed, ironically, for many opportunities to show kids just how relevant the old canonical texts are. If you're teaching *King Lear*, for example, you can bring in HBO's recent *Succession* series or *Empire* on Fox. Recently, we have seen yet another retelling of the Batman story—the feature film *Joker* (Phillips, 2019)—that can easily be linked to Beowulf and Grendel. Yet I routinely encounter teachers who tell me they don't have a Netflix account or "don't watch TV." Even just allowing students to riff off the whole-class text you are reading can lead to an amazingly rich conversation filled with allusions to a variety of texts. This could simply consist of asking the kids to think about what films or shows or videos have similarities with the classroom text. Ironically, this kind of riffing can open kids' eyes to the relatability of traditional canonical texts. The so-called "new literacies" have actually been a boon to "old" literacies. But many teachers seem to fail to realize this, seeing the situation as one of "us vs. them."

I was startled at Ms. Davis's casual attitude about phones because I run into many educators who have not embraced these new ways of reading and writing. Walk in almost any school in North America, and cell phones are to be checked at the schoolhouse door. For many educators, the status quo is apparently worth preserving. At the annual conference of the National Council of Teachers of English, they sell t-shirts with the slogan, "I liked the book better." Even the general public seems to believe that we should "bring back the good old days" especially when it comes to reading and writing. A recent Oscar Mayer ad shows a happy family gathered around a picnic table eating hot dogs. The caption reads: "Family connected. No WiFi needed." The original marketers of the iPad also apparently realized that we are very conflicted as a society regarding new media. So an early advertisement for the iPad offered a free download of A. A. Milne's *Winnie-the-Pooh*, trying to make the screen more palatable by offering a little Pooh bear (Hendrix, 2013).

FLASHBACK AND FLASHFORWARD

As I worked with the Glenville teachers, I reflected back on my own classroom teaching and on other classrooms I had seen and profiled. From my earliest visits to Glenville, I was not seeing the barriers that prevented other teachers from using all kinds of forms of representation. As I met each week with the English teachers, we talked about our favorite instructional strategies. I would sometimes use the advance organizer: "Things we want to see in our classrooms/Things we don't want to see." This was based on a protocol I saw demonstrated once at a school in Calgary, in Canada (Kist, 2005). From the "Things we want to see" list, it was clear from the start that the Glenville English teachers were truly interested in going beyond just improving their test scores to improving the lives of their students, and working toward a goal of fostering student-centered inquiry. The Glenville teachers wanted to see active reading, not passive; ease of moving between different media and forms of representation; and development of student voice in print and other student-produced texts.

The topic of "inquiry" has been at the forefront of discussions of teaching and learning for centuries (Goldstein, 2014; Kliebard, 1986). There have been many models for structuring inquiry-based projects, from writers as varied as Rousseau, who described the teaching of Emile (1762/1979), to Holt, who talked about "unschooling" (Holt, 1967/1995) and Dewey, whose work emphasized the importance of experience and the need for the arts (1902/1990; 1934/1980). Of course, in our field of English/language arts, we have many examples of inquiry-based projects such as the I-Search paper (Macrorie, 1988) and the multigenre paper pioneered by Tom Romano (Romano, 2000). The technology that so many of us are carrying around in our pockets is quite conducive to an inquiry-based approach to learning—we have the ability to curate our own inquiry paths 24 hours a day.

At the same time when we have seen descriptions of exciting inquiry-based teaching strategies, we continue to see urban schools as portrayed as "less than," filled with "at risk" students (Kozol, 1991/2012). Some authors have posited that helping urban kids become conversant in using the "dominant cultural capital" might be the answer to their at-risk-ness (Gorski, 2020). Not all writers who write about school seem to honor and privilege the funds of knowledge that urban students bring to school with them as promoted by Gonzalez et al. (2005). If innovative, inquiry-based, arts-based projects are being used with students, these often seem to be set in afterschool programs (Brass, 2008; Goodman, 2003; Turner & Bailey, 2020) rather than to be integral parts of the school's pedagogy.

Starting with Ms. Davis's innovative link from *The Hate U Give* to athlete protesters to "The Lottery" (Jackson, 1949), I began to realize that the Glenville teachers with whom I was working were walking the walk of a funds-of-knowledge, inquiry-driven, digital-media-and-arts–inclusive teaching philosophy. And they were doing all this during the school day. We began to discuss the usefulness of the curation model to give a name to what they were doing. The first step of curation—helping students become collectors—of themes, of ideas, and of forms of representation was very common in the Glenville classrooms. To help students make connections and to begin to "collect" texts, the teachers were using fairly common instructional strategies in unusual ways. They were doing so in an urban high school and using common everyday screen-based devices, asking students to draw upon their everyday experiences.

I saw the collecting step of the curation process unfolding as Ms. Davis and her students built a text set related to the book and film of Angie

Thomas's *The Hate U Give*. As students read the novel, they were embarking on an inquiry project that relied heavily on YouTube and other online resources while building text sets and having a dialogue related to the theme of speaking out against injustice. Students collected and analyzed multimedia texts as disparate as *I am Malala* (Yousafzai & Lamb, 2013), "The Lottery (Jackson, 1949)," *Things Fall Apart* (Achebe, 1958/1994), and the films *Black Panther* (Coogler, 2018) and *Get Out* (Peele, 2017). Students went on a field trip to see the film version of *The Hate U Give* (Bourne & Thomas, 2018) when it premiered in the fall of 2018 and followed an innovative process of comparing and contrasting the book and the film. During the 2019–2020 school year, they attended the opening day of *Harriet* (Lemmons, 2019) at the local cinema and also watched episodes of *When They See Us* (DuVernay, 2019).

It was evident that the Glenville teachers also had their students create and repurpose. I heard about the internationally acclaimed video documentarian who came to Glenville and co-created a documentary film with Glenville students focusing on the Glenville shoot-out in 1968. I began to see evidence of kids pouring their hearts out to these teachers in various writings and creative projects and reflecting upon their experiences. This was a community of learners, and I was fortunate to become a part of that community of learners as we met each Tuesday to reflect on where we had been and where we were going. We were putting into practice the four parts of curation, as we made associations between texts of different forms of representation, from both so-called "high art" and "low art." This experience has made me go back through my own curated past and bring out my "greatest hits" in the context of this so-called "at-risk" school. This book is essentially a curated scrapbook of our conversations, preserved in APA 7th-edition format.

THE CURATION MODEL

The intent of this book is to add to the needed conversation about school relevancy by offering real-world examples (collected over several years) of culturally responsive teaching (Ladson-Billings, 1995) that is place-based and uses everyday multimodal technology. What is described in this book is not designed to be replicated "with fidelity," to use an overused education management phrase. One of the key characteristics of the curation model as I'm conceptualizing it is its flexibility, its openness and recursiveness. The curation model is a place-based approach by its very nature, and is also global, lending itself to any learning situation, inside or outside of school. The curation model allows students to foreground their own life experiences in a way that traditional school assignments don't emphasize. The assignments described within this book have allowed students to repurpose texts in their own ways within a school setting. Instead of simply answering fact-level comprehension questions about a canonical text, students have been actively curating their own learning.

Of course, the development of digital media and devices such as smartphones has led us into a kind of curation-driven culture in our out-of-school lives, whether we realize it or not. So many of us now photograph everyday events and post to social media or text, sometimes on a minute-by-minute basis. My experiences as a parent has made me see how kids are natural curators—how they love to collect, organize, and repurpose the important texts of their lives. The assignments included in this book demonstrate how teachers (and parents) can help students see value in their everyday mobile literacies and to see how these daily literacies can be curated to better enrich what are already truly rich and productive literacy lives.

The curation model as defined here is a process that both students and teachers follow involving collecting, organizing, repurposing, and reflecting. The idea is inspired by the notion of what a professional curator does in a museum—collecting great works of art and organizing them and presenting them in new ways to an audience. While there are general steps of curation described below, the act of curation is a very individual act, as each learner tries to make sense of the world and begin to form statements about the world from the very beginning of the process. The steps of the curation model are as follows:

COLLECTING

This first step involves recognition and appreciation for elements in the world—a work of art, something in nature, a mathematical equation, or a scientific process, to name just a few. Becoming a collector involves the development of an aesthetic sense, as students gain practice in truly seeing objects and ideas and in responding, positively, negatively, or neutrally.

ORGANIZING

The second step involves being able to see patterns (or not) in what has been collected. This step involves categorization, of course, but also creativity in seeing how ideas, concepts, and objects can be organized in new ways, using new schema. This Organizing step also demands that each student think about the methods of organization that are best for them. What devices and platforms are available and preferred? What naming system makes past collecting accessible, even across disciplines?

REPURPOSING

This third step involves transforming what has been collected into a new whole, most probably exhibited or performed for an audience (but the audience could simply be the student). How has the collecting and organizing suggested something new, either in terms of concept or presentation? How can the collecting and organizing be structured to form narratives and other kinds of exhibitions that serve to represent individual inquiry paths? How do the forms of representation used during the repurposing help us develop new ways of knowing?

Reflecting

This fourth step serves as a pause to think about what has been learned, what growth has occurred as a result of the first three steps, and what might be next goals for curating. What gaps in the learning are there? Where does the learner need to go next? What, finally, has the learner learned? Students find that reflection may be the most important step in the process, as this is the step in which they begin to self-actualize and set their own goals for learning and growth.

The curation model is both old and new—it builds upon a foundation in aesthetics that is centuries old, while it takes advantage of the new literacies often delivered via portable screen-based devices that give us instant access to all that we could possibly want to curate. Somewhat fortuitously, we were able to refine our model in this truly special place; Glenville High seems related to so many touchstones of 20th-century and, now, 21st-century American history, from being the birthplace of Superman to being the site of a speech by Martin Luther King, Jr., to being the location of much work in the area of social justice and racial equality in recent years. And we were witness to students during the last few years who were using their own technology as they constructed meaning from texts in the midst of a world that seemed increasingly chaotic and weighted against them. As they read and viewed not only canonical texts, but also social media and various multimedia texts, students were able to form a kind of running record of their learning in a way that transcended planned curriculum and extended beyond any grading period, semester, or year. During our discussions, it seemed that curation gave us a name and a template for student activities that helped them learn skills that would benefit them as they moved out into the world—skills such as discerning commonalities and differences, learning to look for patterns and contexts, being able to organize and critically repurpose texts, and being able to reflect and be able to think about next steps. Whether or not students intended to further their education after high school, as we developed and worked through various assignments and assessments, we saw signs that students were playing active roles in the world not only through keeping track of their learning but also by being proactive regarding local and national issues.

Now that we are in the midst of a massive shift to remote learning due to the world pandemic, it seems that the skills that were being taught over the last few years at Glenville are fast becoming foundational to the modern American high school experience whether students are at home or in a brick-and-mortar school. It is hoped that this book will help define and give shape to a useful pedagogical approach, no matter the setting. I also believe the projects and assignments described in this book are simple to implement and can easily fit into existing curriculum models, especially in a post-virus world that will be increasingly lived online and aware of the need for culturally responsive teaching.

The next chapter of this book provides an overview of the various components of the curation model and their foundation. The remaining chapters provide illustrations of assignments for each part of the curation model in a way that will benefit all secondary teachers (both preservice and in-service). While this book is set in a historically African American high school in Cleveland, I believe the assignments included here can transcend types of schools and be successful in all kinds of educational environments, in both brick-and-mortar and online settings. Strategies and assessments will be shared with concrete illustrations from my work and the work of the Glenville teachers as examples. Many of the examples are set in the context of doing an in-depth text-set study related to the new classic young adult (YA) book *The Hate U Give* (Thomas, 2017) including inquiry projects and text sets that were constructed related to the book and to activism and protest through the last 5 decades.

The English teachers at Glenville have been busy over the past few years. This book documents their work and does so in the context of a model that can be flexible and adaptable to any learning situation. Through describing the work of the Glenville teachers, the book provides a model for schools that might be searching for answers during these challenging times. This book makes the argument that a model based on the concept of curation can be a powerful option. The book will provide a guide (as well as a call) to teachers and administrators to have the kind of conversations we have had at Glenville since 2018. The idea of "creating a literacy life" has been a helpful way of conceptualizing the work and guiding our conversations. Curation is a kind of catch-all learning-to-learn model, a way of helping kids become consumers and creators in their literacy lives both inside and outside of school. The resulting student-curated digital collections can become the hub for school activities, providing the inspiration not only for self-directed inquiry projects, but also for drafting and publishing their work.

In short, this book provides real-life descriptions and, ultimately, an argument that inquiry-based projects that involve technology can and should be used more often in urban environments. The Glenville teachers have demonstrated that much can happen when teachers go beyond worksheets and cocreate inquiry-based lessons and projects with their students, and when students begin to curate their own learning. Grounded in theories of social justice pedagogy and critical media pedagogy, the curation model operationalizes an inquiry-driven emphasis that builds on students' funds of knowledge. What happens when urban students are allowed and encourage to move beyond pacing guides and curriculum maps? This book will provide documentation of some teachers that have attempted more of a student-centered approach. It's worth noting that the writing of this book coincided with the onset of the COVID-19 pandemic. Much of what is described in this book took place before the onset of the pandemic in March 2020, and some of the plans we had at that time were put on hold. But the Glenville teachers adapted, and I think we discovered silver linings as Glenville switched to using online platforms such as Schoology and Google Classroom, Microsoft Teams and Zoom.

More than ever before, we have the opportunity to fully realize the goal of setting up our kids as lifelong learners.

CHAPTER 1

Curation and Glenville High School

Curation as a metaphor for thinking about literacy offers a structure that can support the many aspects of new literacies research. With its roots in the arts, it appealed to me early, as I have always preferred an arts-based learning perspective rather than an instructional-technology focus when thinking about new literacies. After looking at some recent uses of *curation* and similar terms, I will lay out the research that supports and informs my use of this model.

PREVIOUS USES OF THE TERM "CURATION"

Most of us (unless we are extreme non-savers) are curators in some fashion: We select, we gather, we order and display, and we think about our stuff. Whether we collect vintage Hot Wheels cars (as my son does) or comic books, or rocks, most of us have some kind of collection. And many of us have multiple collections. As Henry Jenkins writes in his recent book, *Comics and Stuff* (2020), "Unlike previous generations, the stuff that matters most to us is often not a matter of inheritance, heirlooms and legacies. Rather, they are frequently elective purchases, items we've chosen because they reflect our own identities, values, and lifestyles" (p. 18).

As young children have shown us, from a very early age they are already quite joyful collectors and even curators of their own learning (Dyson, 2003). Any parent can share stories of discovering their child's collection of objects stuffed in jacket pockets or in closets. And in addition to physical stuff, we now have unprecedented ability to collect texts—both ones created by others and those created by ourselves. We make our own playlists in Spotify and list our own recipe creations in Pinterest. We collect TikToks about beekeeping (as my daughter Mariel does). Anyone who has set foot in even a small comics convention will see grown men and women investing thousands of dollars in collections of graphic novels, costumes, books, art, and souvenirs.

Regarding thinking about curation in schools, we can look at the research related to journaling in schools for parallels to curation. Scholars and teachers have talked about the benefits of having kids keep writers' notebooks (Atwell, 2015; Calkins & Harwayne, 1990; Fletcher, 1996), often in a cross-disciplinary fashion (Glasgow, 1999; McMillan & Wilhelm, 2007). Of course, many of these authors were writing during a time when notebooks could be kept only on paper, so the writers' notebooks as described could not include modes of representation other than text or drawing. And what was being written and collected in these writers' notebooks was often in response to direct prompts from an instructor. Still, there was a kernel of "curation" in these descriptions of writers' notebooks in that students were encouraged to be close observers (perhaps even connoisseurs) of what they were seeing.

As our literacies have become less paper-based, researchers have suggested multimodal or digital activities of selecting and collecting (sometimes describing these as curation), but the resulting digital portfolios were in some cases meant more as tools for educators (assembling a grouping of texts and/ or activities for students or as a tool for reflection) than as a way of learning about the world (Fahey et al., 2007; Oner & Adadan, 2011; Sharma & Deschaine, 2015). Other researchers have described "curation" as a kind of digital "writers' notebook" allowing for students to gather their writings and critiques in various content areas (Beach et al., 2014; Cohen & Mihailidis; Mihailidis, 2015; Tsybulsky, 2020; Walsh-Moorman, in press).

John Potter has used "curation" to focus on identity, looking at how people curate their identities across platforms (Potter, 2012; Potter & Gilje, 2015). These scholars advocate for teaching students how to "curate (their) own online brand" (O'Byrne, 2012). Potter and Gilje (2015) defined "curation" as "a metaphorical new literacy practice which incorporates the collection, production and exhibition of markers of identity through time in both digital production and social media" (p. 123). A special issue of *E-learning and Digital Media*, in 2015, contained mostly ethnographic studies of how young people present themselves to the world via curating their Minecraft knowledge, for example (Dezuanni et al., 2015) or making films (Doerr-Stevens, 2015; Gilje & Groeng, 2015) or going through family artifacts and stories (DeJaynes, 2015).

FOUNDATION OF CURATION MODEL DESCRIBED IN THIS BOOK

For me, however, *curation* is principally a metaphor to guide the teaching and learning process, a means for achieving both student and teacher empowerment, and a way of engaging with texts of all kinds and making meaning of them, making something new out of them, rather than a vehicle for identity formation and self-promotion. The four steps of curation described in this book (Collecting, Organizing, Repurposing, and Reflecting) work best as a learning-to-learn metaphor. That is, curation can be established as a habit of mind (Costa & Kallick, 2008; Maiers, 2012; Wills, 2021) that teachers and learners can look at to unpack their thought processes no matter where the teaching and learning is taking place—in school or out of school, online or in person. Using everyday smartphones, a Netflix account, and access to a variety of YA, canonical, and media texts (and students' and teachers' vast knowledge of both high and low art), a wise teacher can use the curation model to set a foundation for lifelong learning and inquiry.

Over the years that I've been visiting Glenville, it has seemed like thinking about curation allowed me and the Glenville teachers to synthesize many key strands of current literacy research. It helped us to be intentional about what we were doing and to bring together related strands of literacy instruction in a way that is coherent and useful. As I've said, earlier in my career I often didn't have a name for what I was doing. Curation gave us a name and a process for what we were doing. Our conversations weren't dominated by arguments on how to make activities fit into the curation model; the process is recursive, and it's flexible for different situations (including a pandemic). It brings together in-school and out-of-school literacies. It's addictive.

Multimodality and the Arts

My roots in new literacies research lie in the arts. *Curation* is, of course, associated with museums and galleries, places that house art. I started researching new literacies not because of my devotion to the New London Group (1996), but because I felt that riffing in my own ELA classroom, bringing in a variety of kinds of texts for my students to both read and write, seemed to spark thought and engagement for my students and fun for me. I wanted to find out if there were other teachers out there trying these same ideas and, if so, whether others who were trying these ideas felt these efforts were effective. As the Internet came into our lives in the 1990s, I soon discovered that there were indeed other teachers who were using media and new literacies in their classrooms. I was fascinated by theoreticians who were thinking about and writing about these new media. The new literacies concept, involving as it does texts of many modalities, ran parallel with my own ideas about collecting and curating from different genres and media the way a museum curator might.

I Research into new literacies afforded theoretical and empirical support for my desire to incorporate various media into the classroom and the arts into the lives of my students. I wondered how teachers might use the new forms of texts. What might new media look like in the daily lives of "real" classrooms? The teachers I worked with at Glenville had never heard of the New London Group. But they had heard of Megan Thee Stallion, Ava DuVernay, Malcom X, and Angie Thomas. They made space in their classrooms for all of these artists as well as for Shakespeare, Fitzgerald, and Douglass. From the beginning, I saw the Glenville teachers as kindred spirits as they, like me, sought to infuse their classrooms with multimodal texts. I saw the students as kindred spirits, as well, as they seemed adept at navigating, collecting, and organizing many different kinds of texts. This greater multimodality that the new technology has afforded us spoke to me as a classroom teacher, and it still speaks to me as a university (and post-university) researcher.

Even before the Internet, many educators advocated that the arts should not be considered "specials," but should be central to the thinking and learning we do in schools (Eisner, 2002, 2005; Ernst, 1997). Like them, I feel that educators should cherish the ineffable, unplannable characteristics of the arts in our daily classroom practices; the moment-to-moment experiential nature of the arts makes them a perfect fit for teaching and learning, which should be thought of primarily as experiential in nature (Dewey, 1934/1980; Greene, 2001). Indeed, the arts should be an integrated part of everything we teach.

This arts-based way of knowing continues to be researched. The arts have been shown to be a window into helping students with a variety of needs, from learning physics (van der Veen, 2012) to improving reading abilities (Varnon, 1997) to appreciating canonical literature (Michaels, 2009) to general meaning making (Albers, 1997; Leland & Harste, 1994); from helping with composition (McLean & Rowsell, 2015) to aiding critical thinking (Bowen et al., 2014; Rhoades, 2020) and even performing qualitative research (Wasser & Bresler, 1996; Woo, 2008). We have a lot to learn from artists. We should pay attention to the ways that artists think, just as Vera John-Steiner did in her classic *Notebooks of the Mind* (John-Steiner, 1997).

Multimodal assignments have been viewed as a way to increase student engagement and comprehension (Verlaan, 2017); help students compose literary analyses (Doering et al., 2007; Smith, 2019; Srsen & Kist, 2015); improve academic writing (Jocius, 2020); improve argument writing (Howell, 2017); improve revision in writing in general (Batchelor, 2018a); improve research skills (Bailey & Carroll, 2010); support bilingual family literacy programs (Nunez, 2019); explore students' identities (Olan & Pantano, 2020); teach emotional health (Mills & Unsworth, 2017); and teach multimodally during a pandemic (Pantano, 2020). As Smith (2017) writes in her case study of urban 12th-graders working on multimodal projects, "Multimodal composing [is] a complex, dynamic, and varied process mediated by the interaction of multiple factors" (p. 259). We teachers need to include this dynamic method of reading and writing, which has come to dominate our literacy lives outside of schools, in our classrooms.

The good news is that it's never been easier to "read" and "write" multimodally using multiple forms of representation. But then why does multimodal reading and writing still seem to be relatively rare in our class-rooms? One would hope that teachers and schools would be prominently featuring multimodal reading and writing in an environment that banishes hierarchies of representation. But these kinds of options are not always so evident, which was why I was so surprised when Ms. Davis told her students to take out their phones to look things up, and why I was impressed to hear about the film documentary that the Glenville students were making. Kids seem so able to move effortlessly between so-called "high art" and "low art," but I rarely see this celebrated or even acknowledged in schools. Usually, what is known as "high art" (canonical texts such as Shakespeare plays and visual art such as a Monet painting) is prized more highly in schools than so-called "low art" (comic books and graffiti, to name two examples). I did not see that hierarchy in the ELA classrooms at Glenville.

The multimodal element of curation is all about giving kids options and legitimizing collecting, organizing, and repurposing content using different forms of representation. In today's world, students must learn to be collectors and interpreters of all kinds of messages, not only in terms of "arts integration" in school, but as a necessary element of culturally responsive teaching.

I have so frequently seen that multimodal texts can engage students so powerfully with all texts and their meanings. Shannon Davis writes, "I frequently incorporate full movies, movie clips, interviews, trailers, and all kinds of YouTube videos while I teach. The placement of media may come at different times throughout the lesson. For example, prior to starting *The Hate U Give* I show two interviews with author Angie Thomas that shared pertinent information about the book and the significance of its title. For other texts, such as 'The Lottery' by Shirley Jackson and 'Everyday Use' by Alice Walker, there are movie versions available online. To see the events of 'The Lottery' in the film version really engaged my students, sparking immediate discussions. Some clips are used to explore themes from the text. While teaching *All American Boys* (Reynolds & Kiely, 2017) and *The Hate U Give*, an effective media resource to use is a portion from *When They See Us* (DuVernay, 2019) (or any documentary on the Exonerated 5 from New York City). The thematic connection is teaching students about their rights when dealing with law enforcement as minors and other aspects of social justice. Finally, there are older texts such as *Things Fall Apart* (Achebe, 1958/1994), which do not have movie versions available. In cases like these, YouTube has videos that will explore some cultural and historical aspects from the text."

Both Ms. Davis and Mrs. Haynes talk about the powerful experience of taking students on a field trip to a local cinema on the opening day of the film version of *The Hate U Give* (Bourne & Thomas, 2018) in October 2018. Ms. Davis was teaching the book to all her 10th-graders in a general English class. Mrs. Haynes, an intervention specialist, was collaborating with Ms. Davis, and teaching the book to the students in her resource room. Ms. Davis writes, "Several staff members and I took approximately 100 students to see the film on opening day. The students absolutely loved the book, but as several movie trailers began to surface online for the movie, they were anxiously excited. We arrived at the Tower City movie theater, in downtown Cleveland, and the students bought snacks and they were seated. Students had strong reactions to seeing certain parts of the story played out on the screen. Early on in the film, when the tragic incident occurred when a policeman shot and killed the unarmed teen, Khalil, students started to cry."

Mrs. Haynes recalled, "The students were so excited about this book because they were able to relate to so many characters. Some students were able to relate to Starr because they lived in similar communities and were facing the same community issues she was facing on a daily basis. This allowed the discussions in class to be quite real. Students were listening to their peers when they were speaking out. In the middle of September of 2018, we were not that far into the book, so we decided to begin assigning chapters to read at home. Most students completed the homework assignments. October came so quickly, and everyone was becoming more excited than ever because they were anxious to see the movie. Students were completing all assignments and readings so they were able to attend the movie screening. When the final day came to attend the movie, all students were on time for the bus and all students were ready to learn more about Starr, the main character. They were discussing the book on the bus while riding on the freeway to attend the movie. The excitement was definitely in the universe. When we arrived at the movie theater, we let the students be responsible and sit where they wanted so that they would be comfortable while watching the movie.

"During the movie, we heard many quiet conversations. The students were comparing what they read in the book to what they were seeing on the screen. When the scene of Starr protesting for Khalil came on the screen, students were shouting and finally understood her purpose, to be an advocate for people being mistreated by the police. They could see Starr's determination through her actions and the audience became powerful. It just seemed as though the students wanted to protest with Starr. What a moment to watch! As the movie ended with the scene of Starr's little brother holding the gun and pointing it towards the cops, the room became silent. The students felt the emotions from the characters in the scene. One student ran out of the movie theater crying and was very emotional. It was an emotional time for many of the students. But through it all, they gave the movie a standing ovation at the end.

"There were many discussions on the bus when we headed back to school. The students were talking about the movie for days in class and with their other peers who did not attend the movie or read the book. They were promoting the book and movie and letting others know that they should go see the movie soon. During the conversations, it seemed that many students loved the book more than the movie and vice versa. This film experience allowed the students to be aware of the power of their voices and how powerful they can become. In addition, this experience gave us, teachers, the power to use non-traditional material to teach about different issues that arise in teenagers' everyday lives." Ms. Davis adds, "Seeing such a powerful story on the big screen was an unforgettable experience for the students."

In sum, the constant use of multimodal texts culminating with a field trip to see a film enriched the Glenville classrooms just as they had enriched my classroom many years ago. This ability to mix and match forms of representation remains a cornerstone of the curation model.

CULTURALLY RESPONSIVE TEACHING

From my early classroom days of showing films and playing all kinds of music in my classrooms, mixing modes and deviating from the canon, I was doing what I would later learn to call *culturally responsive teaching*. At the time I thought of it, as Ladson-Billings famously said, as "just good teaching!" (Ladson-Billings, 1995). Sometimes I felt that teaching this way was actively subversive, because it led to questioning the power dynamics of schooling by responding to the cultural forces students cared about. (That feeling grew more pronounced as standardized testing became the centerpiece of school reform.)

I well remember first realizing that what I was doing might in some way be thought of by others as wrong or by some to be "subversive." It was during a 2-hour lunch in the 1990s when I was a brand-new curriculum supervisor. Most of my new colleagues were 20 years older than me, and they definitely wanted to enculturate me into their dominant philosophies. I wondered if we would be in sync. We met in a local tavern that was anything but a franchise. It was dark and hazy, back when you could smoke in a restaurant. My new colleagues were excited to have me meet my predecessor—a man who began his teaching career in the 1960s and who apparently had many stories to tell. As we read the menus and sipped our Diet Cokes in a crowded corner booth, I watched Hubert (not his real name) as he watched me. Hubert seemed to have been born in a trench coat. His face was heavily lined, and his eyes were hidden by his thick horn-rimmed classes. I couldn't tell if he liked me or not, as he murmured some pleasantries. But it was very clear after just a few minutes that he had a very pressing message he wanted to deliver to me. He stopped the conversation, and we all leaned in. "Don't ever forget," he rasped, "teaching is a subversive activity." And that is how I was introduced to the concept of teaching as a subversive activity (Postman & Weingartner, 1971).

Although I had not heard of the Postman and Weingartner book, I already felt in alignment with its spirit. Of course, it had been easy for me to be "subversive" back when I was first hired as a classroom teacher. When I was hired, I was given three items: a key to the book room, a list of about 75 assorted paperback book titles I could teach per grade level, and a blank gradebook. That was it. I wasn't given a copy of the official district curriculum until April, and by then it got hardly a glance. That autumn, the book room had ample copies of *Lord of the Flies* (Golding, 1954/2003) and, although that title had an "H" beside it (indicating it was only for Honors), I went ahead and taught it to all my students. We were off and running.

What I was doing during those years wasn't really that subversive—I was teaching from the approved list of titles, using the books in the book room. But I taught what I wanted to teach in the order in which I wanted to teach it. And I filled my classroom with music, art, and pop culture, things I knew would appeal to my diverse students. I taught in an urban, racially diverse, high-poverty school, and when it was time to read *Beowulf*, I linked it to Batman; I played Marvin Gaye's "I Heard it Through the Grapevine" to teach idioms; and we all performed spoken-word versions of Maya Angelou's poetry. This doesn't seem all that crazy now, but no one else I knew was doing these things.

Looking back now on what Postman and Weingartner (1971) were advocating for, they were suggesting going way beyond playing "I Heard it Through the Grapevine" in class. Some of their suggestions seem humorous today (like "Limit each teacher to three declarative sentences in class, and 15 interrogatives," or "Require each teacher to undergo some form of psychotherapy")—one can almost hear the shocked laughter of those reading the book at the time. But their premise was that education can address some major problems that must be addressed to preserve our survival as humans. As of 1971, the schools weren't cutting it. They hadn't helped solve any or even some of our problems. Schools, Postman and Weingartner thought, should be much more subversive than they were to prepare students to be critics of the culture surrounding them. They proposed throwing out the entire curriculum and replacing it with an inquiry-based approach. "The art and science of asking questions is the source of all knowledge. Any curriculum of new education would, therefore, have to be centered around question asking" (p. 81). In their ideal school, the teacher would rarely tell the students what they ought to know, and no single statement would be accepted as an answer to a question. Students should be trained to be "crap detectors." Teaching should be relevant to the learners' needs and realities, so that learners can become critical thinkers ready to face the problems and challenges of the time.

Today's teachers seem to have a lot less room to be subversive than they did back in 1971, or even when I was teaching. As of this writing, we are seeing a heightened level of acrimony at school board meetings about book choices and the perception that K–12 teachers are teaching "critical race theory." Book challenges seem to have come back into style as some parents object to diverse books such as *All American Boys* (Reynolds & Kiely, 2017), *Beloved* (Morrison, 1987), and *Maus* (Spiegelman, 1986). But how can these books not be taught? As Morrell et al. (2013) so eloquently said, "Students who desire social justice must be critical consumers and producers of texts across multiple genres of both traditional and new media" (p. 5). If students don't have access to all kinds of texts from all kinds of perspectives, how will they be enabled to be fully critical members of our society? I think the curation model with its space for collecting and organizing all kinds of texts is more needed than ever because it is automatically culturally responsive in that it disrupts the literary canon, famously dominated by "dead white males." Students are asked to become collectors and even connoisseurs of all kinds of texts, from a diverse roster of artists and writers.

Thankfully, there are many examples in the literature over the last 20 years of teachers who are opening up their classrooms to this kind of "disruption" (Worlds & Miller, 2019) as they embrace culturally responsive teaching, often simply by diversifying the texts that are being read, viewed, and discussed. We've seen examples of teachers using pop culture to reach out to youth of color in the form of digital storytelling projects (Anderson & Mack, 2019), murals (Rivera, 2020); graffiti (Poveda, 2012); hip-hop (Dover & Pozdol, 2016; Kelly, 2019); tagging (MacGillivray & Curwen, 2007); and multimodal essay composition (Ohito and the Fugitive Literacies Collective, 2020). Valerie Kinloch documented the work of two high school students from Harlem who used photography and video interviews to "document the aesthetics of their community and their black situationality (Haymes, 1995) against the backdrop of adult efforts to reclaim artistic value in Harlem" (Kinloch, 2007, p. 42).

And what's good news is that multimodal texts are not just being used as the "spoonful of sugar to help the print go down" (Kist, 2005). Muhammad (2020) includes use of digital stories as a key means of teaching identity development, which is the first component of her model for cultivating genius: "Students are encouraged to use multimodal technology (photographs, video, animation, sound, performance, print, etc.) to capture the dynamics of their lives and identities" (p. 76). Gonzalez et al. (2020) recently described how a multimodal storytelling project in an after-school program situated on the El Paso, Texas/Ciudad Juarez, Chihuahua, Mexico, border, "provided an opportunity for youth to engage the fugitive literacies that they embody, practice, share, and create" (Gonzalez et al., 2020, p. 223).

Of course, Ladson-Billings (2009) provided us with a foundational definition of the goals of culturally relevant teaching—academic success, cultural competence, and sociopolitical consciousness:

> Briefly, by *academic success* I refer to the intellectual growth that students experience as a result of classroom instruction and learning experiences. *Cultural competence* refers to the ability to help students appreciate and celebrate their cultures of origin while gaining knowledge of and fluency in at least one other culture. *Sociopolitical consciousness* is the ability to take learning beyond the confines of the classroom using school knowledge and skills to identify, analyze, and solve real-world problems. (Ladson-Billings, 2014, p. 75)

In a 2014 piece, Ladson-Billings suggests using "culturally sustaining" instead of "relevant," and she portrays a course she taught as including much of the riffing that we have discussed and featured at Glenville: "Our class had aspects of conventional university courses: a syllabus, readings, discussions, and written assignments. Students read work by canonical social theorists, including Bourdieu, Durkheim, Woodson, and Du Bois. But it also had some new and nontraditional elements. We did close readings of what might be seen as alternative texts—hip-hop lyrics, videos of hip-hop artists, and 1960s-era protest poetry. The final assignment was a performance" (Ladson-Billings, 2014, p. 79).

Gay's phrase of choice is "culturally responsive" and she defines it as "using the cultural knowledge, prior experiences, frames of reference, and performance styles of ethnically diverse students to make learning encounters more relevant to and effective for them" (2018, p. 36).

Because screen-based literacies are so popular and in use by most young, diverse students, allowing for expression using new literacies exemplifies this asset-based pedagogy—a key competency in effective teaching of historically marginalized students (Ladson-Billings, 1999; Lopez, 2017; Delpit & Dowdy, 2002). As Herrera (2016) has said, "Teachers dedicated to seeing their culturally and linguistically diverse students succeed in the classroom place the biographies of their students at the center of their practice" (p. 1). Both Herrera (2016) and Muhammad (2020) have urged placing student biographies (memoirs) at the heart of teaching. And given the dominance of multimedia texts in the lives of our students, these biographies must typically be multimodal in design. In allowing and encouraging these kinds of semi-autobiographical multimodal projects with our students, we truly are making our classrooms culturally responsive and transformative. Rivera (2020), for example, discusses a mural project completed at Chicago's Lincoln Park that broadens the perspective of what "composition" can be: "I witnessed a community-based practice that actively interacted with visual rhetoric, oral rhetoric, performative rhetoric, activism, alphabetic composition, and even computer-generated composition as the audience used mobile devices to take photographs and videos of the event to share in social media outlets" (Rivera, p. 121). As she points out, "societies have communicated in an extensive array of ways throughout history, but it wasn't until the rise of digital platforms that academic disciplines began carefully attending to the multimodal aspect of writing, . . . combining alphabetic writing with other modes" (Rivera, p. 121).

In light of the dramatic health-related and sociopolitical events of 2020 and 2021, the debates that have raged over the past 20 years about "new literacies" seem rather quaint. The increased polarization of our society both within the United States and across the entire world has demonstrated just how vital it is that we get this right. For the past couple of decades, if we had been paying attention to the inequities that surround us (rather than focusing on statewide standardized test scores), we would have opened up our classrooms to the devices and texts that our kids are using and reading.

Shannon Davis, one of the Glenville teachers with whom I worked, did not shy away from being culturally responsive. She writes, "One of the more popular media sources used throughout my ELA units on social justice and culture is a poem by Kale Nelson called 'The War on Black Boys.' We watch a clip of Nelson reciting his poem as part of a poetry slam. The poem is his passionate reflection of the war he finds himself in as a young Black man in America. Full of emotion, he confesses his fears. Using powerful metaphors, he details the harsh realities and stereotypes that plague young Black men.

"Generally, I introduce the poem towards the middle of a unit focused on social justice. By this point, the students have encountered characters who have faced varying social justice-related issues, so the poem directly connects to these other texts. After watching the poem at least twice, the students give a subjective statement about the poem. They identify the metaphors that stand out to them. The students write about how the poem relates to various characters from our other texts. Using the poem within the unit has always been effective. Students usually ask to watch the video clip repeatedly. The poem mentions Trayvon Martin, Tamir Rice and Freddie Gray whose murders caused outrage to many. From these names being mentioned, students began to share names of people they know who were murdered, or they share stories of personal encounters with law enforcement. The next time I use this video clip, I plan to have students write their own poems, songs, or raps."

Glenville has a history of not only reading and viewing a variety of kinds of texts within a culturally responsive stance, but producing them as well. Over the past few years, students at the school have worked with a professional filmmaker to produce a film documentary about the Glenville Shoot-out in 1968. Students interviewed residents of the community who remember the events of 1968. This project will be described in more detail in a later chapter.

The resistance to using culturally responsive, multimodal texts in classrooms is all the more strange because we have many examples of young people who have been using their devices (outside of school) to get involved with issues on a global level or to become part of a worldwide community of creators. There are many well-known examples, such as Greta Thunberg's School Strike for Climate change, and the Arab Spring that occurred in 2011 in which young people used social media to protest oppression. But there are also many examples popping up online, including the site Playing for Change (playingforchange.com) which has as its goal to connect the world via music. And the It Gets Better project (itgetsbetter.org) helps LGBTQ youth who are bullied, with its message mostly conveyed via social media. Other young artists use their platforms "simply" to create art. Anne Teresa de Keersmaeker's challenge for people to upload videos of themselves dancing her choreographed dance called "Rosas danst Rosas" is one example, as is HitRecord.org, a site created by actor Joseph Gordon-Levitt, which allows students from all over the world to collaborate on various artworks. Of course, there have been negative and damaging uses of social media performed by young people as well during these last years. And doesn't that fact also support the argument that we need positive school-based digital experiences in school?

My experiences in my own classrooms over the years and my experiences at Glenville have led me to believe that a key foundation for the curation model is to teach in culturally responsive ways. Often, simply allowing students to "read" and "write" in some of their favored forms of representation automatically makes one's classroom culturally responsive.

FANDOM

When students see some of their favorite music and films being used inside school, they often seem shocked or at least a little chagrined. "You mean you know that song, Mr. Kist?" Or "You watch that TV show?" I think one of the key foundational elements of curation is allowing and even honoring *fandom*. Unfortunately, as Henry Jenkins (1992/2013) has written in his classic book *Textual Poachers*, fandom has often had to be defended: "Rejecting media-fostered stereotypes of fans as cultural dupes, social misfits, and mindless consumers, this book perceives fans as active producers and manipulators of meanings. Drawing on the work of Michel de Certeau, it proposes an alternative conception of fans as readers who appropriate popular texts and reread them in a fashion that serves different interests, as spectators who transform the experience of watching television into a rich and complex participatory culture" (Jenkins, 1992/2013, p. 23). It's strange that fandom is seen as "less than," something we do "in our spare time." I've often had conversations with very young fans of some media text, some barely in elementary school. These fans are already very conversant and knowledgeable about whatever they're interested in—Harry Potter, Pokemon, a certain kind of music or fashion. As these fans get older, they participate in fandom activities—going to conventions, participating in online communities and perhaps writing fanfiction pieces. None of these activities have a place inside schools.

I've recently been interacting with various fandom communities outside school. In June 2019, I visited my first full-blown comic con in Denver where I was a featured speaker for the education strand of the conference. The experience of being around so many fans of pop culture was a mind-blowing experience. And I got to meet the Penguin (well, a guy dressed up like the Penguin, the classic Batman villain)! At this event, I rubbed shoulders with some true super-fans, men and women who would think nothing of dropping several hundred dollars or more on some long-sought collectible. The "cosplay" at this event was amazing, as men and women had obviously spent countless hours creating elaborate costumes of their favorite characters, sometimes characters so obscure that they might only exist in a film as a cameo appearance. It was also my first time seeing how photographs are bought and sold at conventions. In the exhibit hall, there was a location where the guest stars would pose for pictures. All of the posing was done behind dividers, presumably so that one couldn't snap a photo of a celebrity without paying for it. There were about 40 different celebrities posing for pictures, including actors from old sitcoms, graphic novel artists, and voice-over actors from a recent video game. Some of the actors at that convention included Christopher Lloyd, George Takei, and Michael Rosenbaum (who played Lex Luthor in the television series "Smallville"). I walked right past Sam J. Jones ("Flash Gordon") who was leaving his booth for a moment. On many levels, this conference seemed more serious in tone than many academic conferences I've attended—instead of chatting about where they were going to eat or the pros and cons of their hotel rooms, I witnessed long conversations held by participants about such important matters as which was the best Robin (to date, there have been five in the comic books) and whether the Mandarain Twist in *Iron Man 3* made sense. These were not casual fans. They had invested not only a lot of money but a lot of time and energy into following their favorites, thinking about them, and debating various issues.

During this same period, I also have been going to car shows due to the fandom of my son Liam, who is nine. Although Liam is too young to have a car of his own, he loves being immersed in car culture, from Hot Wheels and Matchbox cars up to and including the 1965 Ford Falcon owned and lovingly restored by our neighbor. Again, I've been amazed at the knowledge and expertise demonstrated by car collectors. Most of this car wisdom is self-taught on the part of fans who have learned vast amounts of car wisdom quite outside any kind of schooling. As Liam and I wander through rows and rows of cars, we meet collectors who can identify the year and model of a car in seconds. In Liam's rapt study of cars, I am witnessing the genesis of this kind of fan devotion.

Of course, I need to be self-reflective when it comes to fandom. I'm a fan, too. Although I don't believe I have risen to the level of some of the rabid fans I met in Denver or at the car shows, I do put a fair amount of energy into collecting books and music (vinyl and digital). And, of course, as an academic, I've been rewarded over the years, for collecting and, of course, repurposing. Academics' notes, their stacks of photocopies and photos, their walls of books, could all be thought of as curated collections. Over the past few years, I have spent a fair amount of time digitizing many of my paper files and coming up with an organizational system for them on my laptop. I've been collecting and organizing on the topic of curation for over 20 years and this book is a new repurposing of my collecting. Because I've written academically in the area of media literacy, pop culture, and new literacies in general, I've been able to unite my personal book, graphic novel, and music collections with my academic interests. As I have been doing much more online teaching over the past few years, I've noticed that my collecting has come in handy, as my online teaching spaces are, essentially, curations and repurposing of my treasured "greatest hits." In fact, I have to be careful that I'm selective and purposeful, that I don't overwhelm students with every article I've seen on a topic, every clip, every cartoon. That I don't overwhelm them with my fandom.

In his latest book, *Comics and Stuff* (2020), Jenkins continues to stick up for fans: "The human activity of mapping meaning onto objects remains a central aspect of contemporary experience. Our personalities assert themselves at every level, shaping what objects we acquire and how we acquire them, what uses we make of those goods and how much stuff we assemble, and what stuff we get rid of, when, and why" (p. 19). In his earlier book, *Convergence Culture* (2006), Jenkins depicted a fluid top-down, bottom-up flow of content: "By convergence, I mean the flow of content across multiple media platforms, the cooperation between multiple media industries, and the migratory behavior of media audiences who will go almost anywhere in search of the kinds of entertainment experiences they want. . . . In the world of media convergence, every important story gets told, every brand gets sold, and every consumer gets courted across multiple media platforms" (pp. 2–3). I believe that I have participated in this top-down, bottom-up flow of content over the years as I've repurposed my love of pop culture into something new, something "useful"—something that you are reading at this very moment.

One could argue we are living in a golden age of fandom. There has been much growth since the days of the 1970s when there were only the "Trekkies" (fans of the original television series *Star Trek*). We are living in an age in which media texts are packed with allusions and intertextual references, also known as "Easter eggs." For example, most moviegoers know enough to sit through the credits for the brief tag ending that is packed with Easter eggs or allusions to other texts or future films. If you didn't know that, you would have missed Lynda Carter (Wonder Woman from the 1970s television series) showing up in the last post-credit moments of *Wonder Woman 1984* (P. Jenkins, 2020). The bestselling book *Ready Player One* (Cline, 2011) and its film adaptation (Spielberg, 2018) were built around the story of game players searching for these kinds of Easter eggs. And one can make a case that current scripted television dramas are also more dense in plot construction, with many more layers of meaning, than were the old-fashioned crime dramas of the 1970s and 1980s. Some series go on for years with characters often referring to events that happened many years earlier. Fans are supposed to keep up with the allusions and even live-tweet to others who might happen to be watching a live broadcast (another ancient concept of broadcasting).

I felt that I was seeing aspects of fandom in the ELA classrooms at Glenville, particularly in the classrooms of Ms. Davis and Mrs. Haynes, as they continued to riff on *The Hate U Give* for virtually the entire school year. The students were building up various collections related to the themes in the book, focused mainly on some variation of the theme of "student voice." The students were able to link to various media texts and make connections to examples of protest music and examples of strong voices in both fiction and nonfiction. But this kind of fandom seems rare in the schools I visit. Where is the convergence in our classrooms? Where is the love? I often feel that the convergence and the flow stop at the schoolhouse door. Whatever text is being studied is studied in isolation with the questions being asked all intra-text questions. There might be one or two "theme" questions, but there are no associations being made that even the most routine fan might make about another type of source. There are no allusions made even to the text that was being read last week (even when short stories might be grouped together in the same thematically related section of the school-sanctioned anthology).

Some educators have talked about using fan culture, but it seems like the goal is mainly to improve traditional school work (see McConnel, 2019, for a recent example.) Roozen (2009) did argue that we need more studies looking at how vernacular literacies in fan fiction communities mediate disciplinary literacies. Even though the literature is full of case studies of rich fandom literacy lives outside of school, once the school boundary is crossed, fandom seems only to exist as the "spoonful of sugar to make the content go down." There are a few tantalizing examples of research demonstrating the power of fandom. Thomas (2007), for example, followed two girls who participated in highly literate fan fiction communities "to collaboratively construct rich narrative worlds and deeply satisfying friendships" (p. 163). Black (2009) followed English language learners for three years as they took part in online fan fiction communities and found they were not only enacting cosmopolitan identities and transactional social connections; they were also experimenting with genres. Rish and Caton (2011) studied a teacher who facilitated fan fiction writing in schools with the goal of developing more sophisticated writing.

Of course, the traditional secondary school in the United States is not set up to encourage the kind of cross-disciplinary, long-term fandom that most people engage in outside of school. Students are moving from subject to subject all day, with little or no coordination between teachers regarding theme or applicability across disciplines. And within the subject-area instruction, teachers tend to think in "units," moving from a Shakespeare unit to a poetry unit to an argumentative-essay unit, with few references to what was done two weeks ago, much less two months ago. I think the curation model could help students and teachers take advantage of long-term fandom, as students will be encouraged to add to their collections within some learning space, coming up with connections and links across texts for the entire school year and beyond, and creating links across the boundaries of in-school and out-of-school literacies.

BRINGING TOGETHER IN-SCHOOL AND OUT-OF-SCHOOL LITERACIES

Certainly, there has never been a better time to help forge bridges between in-school and out-of-school literacies. Over the past 2 years, as we have been struggling with a worldwide pandemic, the lines between school and home have necessarily been blurred. One benefit of these blurred lines is that parents have been getting an inside glimpse of what takes place in schools to a greater degree than ever before. I speak from personal experience in this regard. My own children took part in remote learning between March and October of 2020, and my wife, Stephanie, and I learned a lot about elementary curriculum as we helped our kids with their various school-related tasks.

From the beginning of this experience, we noticed differences in our three children's workstyles and habits. Because the school district where they attend did not always insist on synchronous (live online) classes, my children had the ability to bounce among schoolwork, listening to music, playing with Hot Wheels, making origami figures, and playing the guitar.

And Stephanie and I let them take advantage of that freedom. We noticed, for example, that our daughters preferred to do their schoolwork first thing in the morning, while our son preferred to take a bike ride before getting down to work. We allowed for that difference in work style. And we enjoyed how they might be accessing a text (music or a video) while completing schoolwork. During remote learning Kidz Bop might help them get their groove on while they're working, and that was okay with us. We are fortunate to live in a 1:1 district (a district in which each child is provided with a take-home device; in our case, it was a Chromebook). Their teachers have made good use of the technology. And even though Kidz Bop might be on in the background, our kids remained busy. We would often see our children recording book talks on FlipGrid, participating in Google Meets, and creating Slides presentations. The day we picked up our kids' Chromebooks from the school (handed to us by the gloved principal through our rolled-down car window), my son soon was playing a math game called Prodigy (prodigygame.com) after which he showed me his Slides presentations on the water cycle and on Ohioan Garrett Morgan, who invented the traffic light. He also watched a video about Harriet Tubman courtesy of his online subscription to Scholastic News.

But, still, we couldn't help noticing that, even when they were home, there was still a kind of disconnect between their at-home literacies and their in-school literacies. There seemed to be a very conscious line drawn in the minds of our kids regarding when they were working on schoolwork and when they were just doing "other stuff" on their Chromebooks. Sometimes the "other stuff" seemed more interesting to us, too. I thought of some of the profiles that exist in the research literature of kids with rich literacy lives outside of school. The two Black adolescent males in Kinloch et al.'s 2017 study "relied on literacy during their out-of-school time to talk back to narratives of failure and to interrogate the belief that education is a great equalizer" (p. 36). Gustavson (2008) profiled the sophisticated literacies of a 15-year-old DJ named Gil: "Gil spun the soundtrack to *Raiders of the Lost Ark*. While experimenting with various voices and sounds on the album, Gil found the sound of a gunshot. Through scratching this sound, he transformed the gunshot into something different—a drum beat. Through the improvisational freedom of reappropriating this sound, Gil took a dominant discourse (gunshot as violent act) and invested it with his own particular inflection (gunshot as rhythm). . . . The art of phrasing to him was the element of surprise, catching the listener off-guard with a quirky or familiar pop culture reference or found sound" (Gustavson, 2008, p. 89). There have been many such profiles of students' rich external literacy lives, including their use of computers in Internet cafes (Cilesiz, 2009); their rich enjoyment of graphic novels (Simon, 2012); and their use of technology to learn the dominant culture (Gilhooly & Lee, 2014; McLean, 2010).

If nothing else, I witnessed the freedom of work habits that my children were able to enjoy during the pandemic. I did a fair amount of the writing of this book sitting amongst my children as they worked on schoolwork via their Chromebooks—or didn't!—at their own pace. As for myself, I've found that my writing has increasingly been done wherever and whenever I can, as I watch the Cleveland Browns win a game (amazing), or an old movie on TCM, or some awards show. I'm finding that I seem almost to prefer a lot of activity (including consumption of various texts) while I'm writing.

Often, it is only afterschool programs that allow students to work in multimodal forms in their own ways, including creating videos (Brass, 2008; Goodman, 2003, 2018), music (Kinney, 2012), magazines (Nichols, 2008), or digital stories (Pleasants, 2008). In an alternative school, this freedom of work might be possible during the school day (Schofield & Rogers, 2004).

The curation model allows students to draw upon their at-home literacies for their in-school work, making their classroom reading and writing experiences more authentic. It's a two-way street: The curation model can also extend useful critical literacies skills gained at school into home reading and writing experiences. Especially during the 2018–2019 school year at Glenville, I felt like I was seeing a curation that extended beyond the school day, performed around the book *The Hate U Give*. There was a conscious effort on Ms. Davis's and Mrs. Haynes's to extend the themes of that novel, especially in terms of student voice, so that that students were talking about texts they had seen outside of school and bringing them into conversations in the classroom. There was even the field trip to the local cinema in which students were physically taken beyond the school boundaries. During the 2019–2020 school year, another Glenville teacher, Keisha Davenport, did a project in which students mapped how and where they got their information about COVID-19, dramatically bringing into the classroom their outside-the-classroom literacy lives. This project also asked students to think critically about the texts they were encountering; this critical literacy stance is a key foundational piece of the curation model.

CRITICAL LITERACY

Embedded in the task of any curator is the notion of *criticism*. The curator must be a critic while sorting through the various texts, studying them, and ultimately repurposing them into some new form—an exhibit, an analysis, or even a new work of art. The idea of criticism is implicit through each step of the model and perhaps reaches its height at the end when the curator must take a hard look in the mirror and reflect upon the work done thus far.

Based on the foundational work of Freire (1970/2000), critical literacy proponents suggest that we need to help kids understand the power dynamics that exist within all kinds of media messages. As Rogers (2002) defined it, "Critical literacy stems from discourse theory, critical linguistics, and poststructural theory and assumes the social world is composed of discourses that are inherently unequal" (p. 774). A teacher who is teaching their students according to a critical literacy perspective is helping the students "crack the code" of the subtextual meanings of various texts (Luke, 2000).

Critical literacy scholars are concerned that many young people are just skimming the surface when they engage with media. They are worried about kids who are sending 100 texts a day but are not really engaging with media in a critical way. And what about those young people who are completely tuning out? Should we be comforted by that tune-out? The Oscar-winning film *Boyhood* (Linklater, 2014), shot over 12 years, depicted a boy's life over 12 years; towards the end of the film, the main character talks about how he has shut down his Facebook account because he wants to connect with people face to face. My own experience has shown me that some so-called "digital natives" are, similarly, not interested in technology or use it just at the bare minimum level. Many of the students I currently encounter seem to be more resistant to technology than they were 10 years ago. I consistently have students say things like, "I love the smell of books," and "I detest Twitter." Others have said, "I'm not tech savvy," "I'm so glad this course isn't about technology," and "I'm sick of sitting in front of a computer." One could argue that students who are disconnected need critical literacy skills just as much as those wired kids, if not more. The tech avoiders are at risk of being co-opted or disenfranchised.

Meanwhile, much of what happens in English language arts courses drones on, with an emphasis on fact-level questioning after listening to a book on tape for several weeks. Sadly, this is not a new situation. Dewey criticized schools for this kind of irrelevant teaching over one hundred years ago: "There is very little place in the traditional schoolroom for the child to work. The workshop, the laboratory, the materials, the tools with which the child may construct, create, and actively inquire, and even the requisite space, have been for the most part lacking. The things that have to do with these processes have not even a definitely recognized place in education" (1900/1990).

When one thinks of a museum curator, I think it's safe to say that one thinks of a person who has a certain level of discernment. It wouldn't be much of a museum if the curators who worked there just randomly collected any piece of art. The collecting a curator does should be purposeful and critical. There has to be some organizing principle, some thinking must go on, and those are critical activities. We have had glimpses of what this kind of critical literacy teaching might look like in schools, as kids have been taught to scrutinize websites (Crovitz, 2007); customer ratings and reviews (Rice, 2007); fashion magazines (Skinner, 2007); film (Hodges, 2010); words and images found in 9/11 media (Staples, 2008); advertising (Cuff & Statz, 2010; Gainer et al., 2009); award-winning children's literature (Heffernan & Lewison, 2009); urban fiction (Gibson, 2010); and theater (Rozansky & Aagesen, 2010). This type of critical literacy teaching has been tried with language learners (Choudhury & Share, 2012; Huang, 2011); and with marginalized students (Campano et al., 2013). Often, there is a global education thrust to critical literacy activities (Albers et al., 2016; Kist, 2013; Myers & Eberfors, 2010).

The teachers at Glenville showed me that it is possible to work toward this critical literacy thrust on a small, localized level, one day at a time. Many have written about how innovations are often slow to catch on in any field (Gawande, 2013; Gladwell, 2002; Kuhn, 1962/1996). There is usually some kind of "great leap forward" that leaves the predominant theory or theories in the dust. My work at Glenville has spanned the onset of the pandemic and increased racial and political polarization in this country. Will the mind-blowing events of 2020 and 2021 be the seismic jolt that we need to shake up traditional education? If so, there is no time to lose. Let's hope that we are not going to cling to outmoded practices in a time when it is crucial to let them go. Students who are not able to navigate Twitter intelligently, for example, or write a text with hyperlinks, are going to be marginalized before they even get started in life. And students who are not taught in culturally responsive ways are going to continue to tune out, seeing school as increasingly irrelevant and meaningless. Beyond economic marginalization, young people are going to need to be able to see the relevancy of the school day, navigating the in-school literacies as they navigate out-of-school literacies, so that they can achieve a basic quality of life. In an age of branding, even, of infants (Klein, 1999/2009), we need to start early helping kids go beyond decoding alphabet letters to decoding the situation in which a text has been created and the context in which it is designed to be read.

In the chapters to follow, the curation model is presented as a structure for tapping into the funds of knowledge that all students bring to school, forging more unity between in-school and out-of-school literacies. As teachers and parents search for what the "new normal" might be regarding teaching and learning during these troubled times, curation might be the ideal metaphor that allows students to do authentic work, in multiple forms of representation and in ways that transcend the boundaries of the schoolhouse door.

CHAPTER 2

Collecting

This first step involves recognition and appreciation for elements in the world—a work of art, something in nature, a mathematical equation, or a scientific process, to name just a few. Becoming a collector involves the development of an aesthetic sense, as students gain practice in truly seeing objects and ideas and in responding, positively, negatively, or neutrally. How do we know what is worth collecting? What are the criteria that each person develops to aid in making those decisions?

As discussed previously, a curator is traditionally a person who works at an art museum, helping to build the collection of art and figuring out the most meaningful way to display the museum's holdings. Many of the students at Glenville (and most places) are walking around with all the technology they need to be curators of their own learning, especially as communities have ramped up access to highspeed internet in response to the pandemic. They have space to organize their findings and to display them. The pandemic pushed school districts to equip schools and communities with the devices and services needed to "do school" online. Schools and various nonprofits in many localities are working together with a new sense of urgency to lessen the "digital divide."

Now the fun can begin. The Collecting stage is the part of the process that involves recognition, acquisition, and usually a strong component of joy. I don't mean to suggest that the other steps of curation aren't fun. But this is the really happy part of the process, when students and teachers are finding commonalities between all kinds of texts, existing in the experiential moment of attending to a text in a meaningful way (Greene, 2001). This celebration aspect of curation is something I often saw at Glenville, even in faculty meetings when Jacqueline Bell, the principal, would play her playlist of Motown hits of the '60s and '70s as a prelude to the meeting. There was also daily music accompanying the morning announcements.

One day at Glenville, as Ms. Davis was beginning discussion of *Things Fall Apart* (Achebe, 1958/1994), she asked the students to describe two or three of their family traditions. This was in response to a scene in *The Hate U Give* that features one of the family traditions in Starr's family. Ms. Davis talked about one of her own family's traditions on New Year's Day: "A man has to come in the door first for good luck." Students were willing to share some of their own family traditions. In a follow-up question, Ms. Davis asked "How would you describe the culture of your neighborhood?" Ms. Davis listened to some answers and then asked the provocative question: "Why do people continue to follow traditions even when they are not beneficial to people?" And then another: "Why are some people scared to speak out against wrongdoing and injustices?" After a few minutes of this interesting discussion, Ms. Davis opened up YouTube and showed a 1969 film version of Shirley Jackson's "The Lottery" (Encyclopedia Britannica, 1969). I felt that I was witnessing a fairly effortless collecting of multiple texts related to a central theme (looking at raising one's voice in the face of societal pressures). Ms. Davis was modeling a habit of mind (Costa & Kallick, 2008; John-Steiner, 1997) that is the foundation of becoming a curator—learning to observe and make connections across texts even as one is collecting them. Of course, the first step is simply to help get kids to see. The assignments described in this chapter trend around the concept of observing with all five senses—really seeing, hearing, and reading deeply— and then collecting.

Many of the new literacies units I've seen over the years and at Glenville start with getting kids to assemble various texts and compare-and-contrast them. How do we help our students become collectors? How do we help them become connoisseurs? How do we really get them to see and be observers? And this last question implies the need for a kind of "Aesthetics 101"—helping students understand general principles of the aesthetic experience as they move about the world around them.

AESTHETICS—HELPING KIDS LEARN TO SEE AND HEAR

Before one can collect anything, one must truly see what is being collected. Rosenblatt (1978) famously brought the idea of aesthetics into the ELA world, making aesthetic reading one of two components of reader response (in addition to "efferent" reading, in which the reader is focused on taking something from the text). "In aesthetic reading, the reader's attention is centered directly on what he is living through during his relationship with that particular text" (as quoted in White & Lemieux, 2017). As Greene defined aesthetics, it's "the term used to single out a particular field in philosophy, one concerned about perception, sensation, imagination, and how they relate to knowing, understanding, and feeling about the world" (Greene, 2001, p. 5).

Formal Aesthetic Protocols

There are many formal protocols for developing an aesthetic sense, sometimes set out by museums or concert halls to help audience members get the full enjoyment out of the "high art" that they are seeing. Markovic (2012) suggested three components of aesthetic experiences: "fascination with an aesthetic object (high arousal and attention), appraisal of the symbolic reality of an object (high cognitive engagement), and a strong feeling of unity with the object of aesthetic fascination and aesthetic appraisal" (p. 1). Most formal aesthetic protocols are, indeed, divided into these kinds of categories—observing (fascination) and appraisal. There are many different conceptualizations of what an aesthetic experience is, but the essence of aesthetics is that we humans are responding meaningfully to a text or object or experience. And what is sometimes challenging for plan-happy educators is that this kind of aesthetic response is highly individualized and unpredictable. As Maxine Greene wrote: "We are interested in education here, not in schooling. We are interested in openings, in unexplored possibilities, not in the predictable or the quantifiable, not in what is thought of as social control. For us, education signifies an initiation into new ways of seeing, hearing feeling, moving" (Greene, 2001, p. 7).

Even though true aesthetic response is necessarily of the moment, there are certainly conditions that teachers can foster that facilitate aesthetic response. Even though one can enjoy a text without being trained to do so, there are some skills that can be taught to aid the aesthetic experience. As Berghoff and Borgmann (2007) wrote, "Mediating meaning in the arts requires both the skill of the artist to construct powerful metaphors and the skill of the viewer to construct meaning from the metaphors. Without the requisite skill of both artist and viewer, the dialogue fails" (Berghoff & Borgmann, 2007). Most protocols of aesthetics involve the steps of first seeing and noticing and then reacting.

But we have to be careful not to kill the experience by giving students some fixed rubric to follow. As van Leeuwen (2018) has pointed out, in many cases in the past aesthetic pleasure and meaning making have too often been artificially separated. Interestingly, van Leeuwen points to new media as helping the cause of unifying the aesthetic experience: "Advertising and branding had already begun to reintroduce aesthetics into everyday functional communication, to play with language in multimodal and creative ways, exploiting the affordances of typography and color, appealing to pleasure, and often transgressing linguistic norms (for instance, spelling rules) as well as social norms (for instance, through sexual allusions). Today, digital writing technologies such as Word and PowerPoint go to great length to encourage computer users to aestheticize their writing" (van Leeuwen, 2018, p. 286).

Close Reading of Media

Rather than get super-formal with students about aesthetics, the Glenville teachers and I started by simply immersing the students in various texts and giving them the tools to realize what they were doing by observing and reacting. As described earlier, the teachers made use of field trips to the cinema, discussing the affordances of film in contrast to print. I have always taken field trips to museums, including the Cleveland Museum of Art and the Akron Art Museum. As the pandemic moved us online, we relied more on virtual experiences of art such as the Cleveland Museum of Art provides with its free ArtLens app (clevelandart.org/artlens-gallery/artlens-app). Simply downloading this app to one's phone allows the user to find and manipulate any piece of art the Museum owns, organized chronologically and thematically. As their website proclaims: "Turn your smartphone into a pocket guide to the CMA. . . . Use it as a companion within the museum, or as a way to explore and create from home" (Cleveland Museum of Art, n.d.). While I did not overly structure our visits (either in-person or virtual), I did provide students with a series of debriefing questions to consider as they interacted with various works of art. Some of these questions were adapted from Bean and Moni's (2003) critical literacy discussion prompts. But many of the questions simply got at: What objects did the students like and why?

DEBRIEFING AESTHETIC QUESTIONS

- What work(s) of art did you most enjoy? What was it about them that made you notice and enjoy them? Write down as many details as you can about the work of art.
- What work(s) of art did you most dislike? What was it about them that made you notice and dislike them? Write down as many details as you can about the text.
- Do you notice any trends running through your likes or dislikes?

Choose one work of art to answer the following questions:

- Where does the text come from (its historical and cultural origin)?
- Do you accept how this text is positioning you as a viewer and/or reader? If not, what other positions might there be for reading this text?
- Who gets to speak and have a voice in the text and who doesn't?
- How else might these characters' stories be told?

(Inspired by Critical Literacy Questions from Bean & Moni (2003)

I have noticed over the years that students are able to carry on quite a spirited discussion when using the above questions in relation to works of visual art. It often seems that students are able to articulate their own aesthetic sense more clearly in response to a work of visual art or a film or song than in response to a novel or a short story. Perhaps they feel less free to react emotionally to written material, with its official school context. I can't be sure. But it prompted me to get students used to this practice with films or songs or visual art, items that drew a strong emotional reaction, before asking them to do the same with class texts.

Certainly, the Glenville teachers saw this almost visceral response at the cinema as the students watched both the film version of *The Hate U Give* and, one year later, the film *Harriet* (Lemmons, 2019) projected on the big screen. I also saw many uses of film within classroom instruction. Ms. Davis used films such as *First Day Back* (Plair, 2019), a short fiction film focusing on students who raise their voices when returning to school after a school shooting; *Skin* (Nattiv, 2018) a short fiction film that portrays a racially motivated assault, witnessed by two children; and *After Parkland* (Lefferman & Taguchi, 2019), a documentary about the aftermath of the Florida school shooting. Ms. Davis adds, "I enjoy showing interviews with the authors as well as background on their relevant themes. For example, students watched two interviews with *The Hate U Give* author Angie Thomas, giving a brief synopsis of the book as well as an explanation of the book's title in a short clip on YouTube." The responses she got to these film clips were reminiscent of the response that I got years ago when showing Chaplin's *The Kid*—responses I would characterize as deeply engaged, attentive, anxious, and amused.

One of the ideas I shared with the teachers at Glenville is an idea I've been using for years that I learned from noted media educator Frank Baker (Baker, 2017). I show film clips and go through a close-reading exercise. Again, it seems that students are able to do a very close reading of a film clip when they do not seem so adept at doing close readings of a work of literature. For this activity, I pick out a 3- to 4-minute scene and first have students watch it with no direction other than to watch it. Often, I choose the opening 4 minutes of the first episode of the television series *Lost* (Abrams et al., 2004–2010). This scene sets the stage for the entire series which takes place on a beautiful island in the aftermath of a plane crash. Before viewing the clip the second time, I break the class up into small groups and give each group one element of the film to watch for—cinematography, for example, or sound effects or costuming. Each group is only to listen or watch for that one element as I play the scene again. Once the second viewing is finished, each small group identifies one or two times in the scene in which there was some noticeable application of their element. For example, the sound effects group might notice an explosion or crowd noise or crashing surf. The class

---

FILM CLIPS TO USE WITH CLOSE-READING EXERCISE

(All of these clips are available online for free, as of this writing.)
Opening Scene of Episode One of *Lost* (Abrams et al., 2004-2010)
    https://www.youtube.com/watch?v=xrkFsSgp6MI
Hair Love (Cherry et al., 2019) https://www.youtube.com/watch?v
    =kNw8V_Fkw28
Arbogast (Martin Balsam) meets Mother from *Psycho* (Hitchcock, 1960;
    stop scene before it gets violent) https://www.youtube.com/watch?v
    =5bieliX5KLQ
Silent: A Short Film (Dolby Laboratories, 2014) https://www.youtube.com
    /watch?v=KA6azZALMiE
Paperman (Kahrs, 2012) https://www.youtube.com/watch?v
    =XrqSF2OOz_M

---

watches the film clip a third time. During this third playing of the scene, each group must yell out "Stop!" and explain why their element has become noticeable. While the scene is stopped and they point out a costume element or a camera placement choice, we talk about how artistic choices are intentional, that it wasn't an accident that we were seeing a closeup of an actor's eyes, or that an actor was seen running from left to right across the screen. We also talk about affordances of film—for example, that a very low bass rumble produced by string instruments or a piano can evoke feelings of fear, or how colors can signify some deeper intent, how red suggests passion, for example. When doing this exercise with students, I often see "the lightbulb go on," as they realize they are learning a kind of secret code, that watching films isn't (only) for entertainment, that we can look at a film in much deeper ways. We talk about the fact that they are doing a close reading and that close readings can be done of any kind of text. Of course, we can still watch a film purely for entertainment reasons, but that sometimes being a close reader can enhance our enjoyment of a text. For example, when I use the opening scene from *Lost* (Abrams et al., 2004–2010), students are amazed when they realize the white dog who rushes through the opening scene is an allusion to the white rabbit in *Alice in Wonderland* (Carroll, 1865/2019).

Often, after we have finished the close reading of film clips, I move on to doing close readings of music. I choose pieces of music with no lyrics, so we are looking at them abstractly, with no verbal cues regarding what the music is "about." We make the transition from talking about techniques that filmmakers use to techniques that musicians use, including instrumentation, tempo, and dynamics. I ask questions such as "What instrumentation did the composer use in this song to suggest mood?" and "What about tempo?"

> ### MUSIC CLIPS TO USE WITH CLOSE-READING EXERCISE
>
> (All of these clips are available online as of this writing.)
> Theme from *On Golden Pond* by Dave Grusin (Rydell, 1981) https://www
> .youtube.com/watch?v=1sJ2ohqt-us
> Theme from the animated series *Batman Beyond* by Kristopher Carter
> (Kane & Finger, 1999-2001) https://www.youtube.com/watch?v
> =k8Y5SLcBJks
> "Spring" from Vivaldi's *Four Seasons* https://www.youtube.com/watch?v
> =6LAPFM3dgag
> "La Enganadora" by Rubén González (from the album *Introducing Rubén
> González*) https://www.youtube.com/watch?v=OQmOFcy_HkM&list
> =RDOQmOFcy_HkM&start_radio=1

I have sometimes expanded this activity to look at pieces of visual art. When we look at visual art, we look at color and line and figure placement. We try to tease out all the techniques that visual artists use to communicate. And then, at last, we move on to prose. We talk about the sounds of the words, sentence construction, and dialogue. Sometimes I begin the print exercises with a picture book, *Charlie Parker Played Be Bop* (Raschka, 1997), which uses nonsense words to approximate the sound of bebop jazz. Then we read aloud some poetry or a paragraph of prose that reads a bit like prose poetry. I ask, "What are the techniques that authors use to evoke feelings as you read and hear their work?"

I tend to repeat this exercise over several weeks, and I try to avoid always ending with print, because I feel that privileges print. I don't want it to seem like I'm only doing these close-reading activities to serve print comprehension. And I ask students to bring in their own film clips, pieces of music, or visual art to "read." I've gotten some great examples to use with future students, including especially some music pieces that were previously unknown to me.

Ms. Davis does a close-reading activity called "Symbol Hunting." She starts by showing a short film called "Symbolism in Film" by commercial filmmaker Chris Constantine (https://www.youtube.com/watch?v =WhijmmePlU8). This provides an overview of how text authors use symbolism to communicate. And then she shows the "84 Lumber Super Bowl Ad" from 2017 (https://www.youtube.com/watch?v=nPo2B-vjZ28). In this ad, a mother and daughter are shown walking a long distance, attempting to enter the United States, apparently from some southern country. When they have almost reached their destination, they come face to face with a huge wall. At the moment of their greatest desperation, the daughter pulls out a little handmade American flag to cheer her mother—the symbol of what they're trying to achieve. The tag line is: "The will to succeed is always welcome here."

She also shows the Audi Super Bowl "Daughter" ad from 2017 (https://www.youtube.com/watch?v=Jk6VIswOCmU). In this commercial, a girl is shown taking part in a rough-and-tumble Soap Box Derby race down a long hill strewn with obstacles. As the girl jockeys for position and, ultimately, wins the race, we hear a male voice-over: "What do I tell my daughter? Do I tell her that her grandpa is worth more than her grandma? Or that her Dad is worth more than her mom? Do I tell her that, despite her education, her drive, her skills, her intelligence, she will automatically be valued as less than every man she ever meets? Or maybe I'll be able to tell her something different." And then the father and daughter walk off into the distance and get into an Audi with the tag line now visible: "Audi of America is committed to equal pay for equal work. Progress is for everyone." In this ad, the brand new Audi is apparently supposed to be a symbol of gender equality. Ms. Davis unpacks the use of symbolism in these ads. She then transitions to *The Hate U Give* and asks students to think back over what they have read and identify two symbols from the book. For each symbol they identify, students are asked, "What role/part does the symbol play in the book/movie? What is your interpretation of this symbol? What is the deeper meaning of this symbol? Cite textual evidence from the book to support your answer." Over the years that Ms. Davis has been doing this symbolism lesson, she has seen students grow in their abilities to pick out underlying meanings of texts.

Critical Reading of Media

Ms. Davis's Super Bowl ad exercise demonstrates the overlap between the teaching of aesthetics and the teaching of critical literacy within the Collecting stage. As students are learning to do close readings of texts as they collect them, these close readings should include *critical* readings of texts as well. This spirit of criticality really is imbued in the entire curation process, as students get practice thinking about the subtexts beneath the texts. One exercise I have done at this early stage is simply to show television scenes from different decades that portray women. Thanks to YouTube, I've been able to find telling scenes from such programs as *I Love Lucy*, *Laugh-In*, *All in the Family*, *Roseanne*, *Seinfeld*, and *Nurse Jackie*. We watch each scene and then, in small groups, use my critical literacy questions to discuss how these texts have positioned women over the years, in regard to career portrayals, leadership, and family roles. As with the close reading described above, I have found over the years that students who are new to these kinds of questions seem more able to answer them when we are looking at film and video portrayals than if we had started with print. Of course, the goal is to build facility with asking and answering these kinds of questions no matter what text is being read or viewed.

Once we have done a few in-class activities related to media portrayals, I ask students to go out into the vast media landscape and find their own examples of media portrayals of certain characters or activities. Following a suggestion by Trier (2006), I have assigned students to search for media portrayals of literacy. Quoting from my assignment sheet, "Your task is to find examples of literacy in pop culture and contribute them to our class wiki. Whenever you find a clip/picture/sound file/other example in pop culture, you should upload it to our class wiki along with a brief paragraph describing it. Our essential question will be, what trends do we see in how the creators of pop culture (film, television, journalism, music, fashion, etc.) view literacy?"

I often saw learning stations being used in the Glenville ELA classrooms to provide some context for various media texts the students were reading or viewing. As Mrs. Haynes describes, "Students rotated through four stations, which each included tasks to complete in the allotted time. The first station was based on a brief graphic novel, 'The Jackson Sit-In' (Thompson & Rath, n.d.). In the second station, students read an informational article on crime and punishment in the United States, focusing on teenagers who commit adult crimes (Smith, 2018). The third station required students to look at the lyrics of the song 'This is America' by Childish Gambino (Glover et al., 2018). At the final station, the students analyzed pictures from racist beatings and segregated events in history (one of which—the Emmett Till lynching—is mentioned in the book). The students wrote and then discussed their viewpoints on the pictures.

"At the learning station for the song 'This is America,' I enlarged the lyrics to display on posterboard to hang on the wall. Students were first to read the lyrics, one stanza at a time, and identify what each stanza meant from their own knowledge and experiences with no more than three sentences. Then the students were to write how each stanza related to the book *The Hate U Give*. The students wrote their answers next to each stanza on the posterboard. If students made mechanical errors, they had space to make corrections. This station allowed students to understand how artists find their voices (as Starr Carter did) through music and their lyrics.

"Before we began the rotation through the learning stations I played the video of 'This is America.' We reviewed the video twice and had a discussion as a whole group before we went into the learning stations. This acted as a hook for the lesson. I wanted the students to ask questions that could be researched later on as an assignment after the learning stations were completed.

"When students were rotating throughout the learning stations, they were able to view other students' comments and how they reacted to each issue faced in each station. Students were able to gather after each class and discuss something new they learned that day, from the activities or from the responses from their peers. When students saw others participating in the discussion, they were able to find confidence to use their voices."

While performing each task, students were motivated and engaged. The conversations were rich, as each station added new texts and new ways to think about student voice.

As will be described at greater length in Chapter 4, the Glenville students also were active producers of texts as well as consumers, and this was true even during the Collecting stage. For several years, some Glenville students participated in a documentary film project that focused on the Glenville shoot-out in 1968. As part of the process of making this film, students were collecting new material in the form of interviews of people in the community who had witnessed the upheaval in 1968 as well as the fallout that has continued to this day. During the Collecting stage, a simple yet profound activity is simply to assign students to interview someone in the community who is older than themselves about some historical occurrence. Students should ask questions aiming "to find some aspect of history. The goal is to have you find some aspect of his or her life fascinating and to learn as much about a specific time or place as possible" (Mathieu, 2014, pp. 142–143). Asking students to do this kind of interviewing seems to automatically spring them into curator mode as they see themselves collecting important stories that no one, perhaps, has collected before.

I'm including this oral history project in this Collecting chapter, because I think it's important to stress how recursive and messy this curation model can be. With the curation model, we break down the old binary that says students are either reading or writing, either receiving or making, and may even ask them to write what will be read. Collecting oral histories might also "fit" into the repurposing stage. During the collection stage, there might be the need to go out and find new material, even if that means generating it yourself.

Text Sets and Intertextuality

Essentially, this chapter proposes asking students (and teachers) to form what are known as "text sets." The more deeply students engage with texts, the more they really see them, the more they are able to put them together in some kind of "set" and begin to think about them intertextually. What I saw with the Glenville teachers I would call riffing or remixing, putting texts together in new and interesting ways. And it was what I was doing years ago in my own classroom without realizing what I was doing. I was bringing in multimedia texts because I wanted to share my own joy experiencing the texts with my students.

There are many articles describing the use of text sets, including text sets to teach transcendentalism (Ruggieri, 2002), war stories (Fischer, 2006), global literature (McCaffrey & Corapi, 2017), and YA literature (Eisenbach et al., 2018) and to promote agency and social justice (Batchelor, 2018b) and critical inquiry (Coombs & Bellingham, 2015). Text sets are used in subject areas beyond ELA, too (Thompson, 2008).

As Jason Griffith (2018) writes, "When a song I'm listening to connects to a book I'm teaching, which makes me think of an image that would help tie the two together, I'm curating a potential text set for my students. However, I can continue to develop, grow, and adapt the set with new texts I discover that connect meaningfully, and students can curate their own related texts as well. In the semester following my original pairing of Lamar, Lady Justice, and *All American Boys*, we added Jay-Z's video op-ed from *The New York Times*, "The War on Drugs Is an Epic Fail" (Carter et al., 2016), and scenes from Ava DuVernay's documentary *The 13th* (Barrish, 2016), each of which contributed new dimensions to our discussion on racial disparities in modern justice and also created fresh avenues for discussing interrelated genres and modalities of texts. By engaging in this process of constantly curating contemporary, quality, and multimodal texts, teachers have a tool to address some of the inherent problems in having to teach even outdated canonical novels" (pp. 39–40).

Over the years, this kind of riffing on a text has been referred to as teaching intertextuality (Fischer, 2006; Semali & Pailliotet, 1999), or it is sometimes referred to as "remixing" (Gainer & Lapp, 2010a; Lankshear & Knobel, 2006). "Literacy as remix positions readers as active meaning-makers who blend understandings based in prior knowledge and experience with new information as they construct new understandings from textual transactions" (Gainer & Lapp, 2010b, p. 58). A curator is an active collector, not a passive collector. There is a purpose to examining all of these texts in an intertextual way. When students collect a group of texts that they see as connected, and look at them in relationship to each other, they begin to act as curators, seeing relationships between texts that they might have never considered to be related.

In February of 2020 just before everything was shut down, I was in Ms. Davis's room when she was deep into her main text, *Things Fall Apart* (Achebe, 1958/1994). The class was beginning to discuss the beginning of Chapter 13, which starts with a depiction of a funeral. "Somebody was dead. The cannon seemed to rend the sky. . . . The faint and distant wailing of women settled like a sediment of sorrow on the earth. Now and again a full-chested lamentation rose above the wailing whenever a man came into the place of death. He raised his voice once or twice in manly sorrow and then sat down with the other men listening to the endless wailing of the women and the esoteric language of the *ekwe*" (p. 120). Ms. Davis stopped at this point, and began to show a YouTube clip: "This Traditional Nigerian Wedding is So Beautiful" (https://www.youtube.com/watch?v =th7yTXQpqy0).

After a few minutes, she stopped the video and asked "Do you all see similarities to what we've been reading?" The students offered several suggestions. She then asked them to brainstorm things they see at a funeral today. Before long, the board was filled with characteristics of funerals. Several kids referenced other fictional representations of funerals, either in film or on the page, and soon they had the beginning of a text set. At one point, Ms. Davis said as kind of an aside, "Every book I have has death."

On the screen I see a tweet Ms. Davis is projecting, "Let's celebrate the men & women who were bullied & sprayed & abused fighting for equality, but aren't in history books #BlackHistoryMonth." During a break, a student asks Ms. Davis if he can take a copy of the Achebe book home with him. I have found one of the most ironic byproducts of this kind of riffing and building of text sets in class is that it tends to get kids more hooked on reading print. Once relevance is demonstrated, through the building of all kinds of texts within the set, there is more of a willingness to engage with books.

Teachers like Ms. Davis seem to be able to do this riffing naturally, so that the class always seems to be engaged in kind of a perpetual "Six Degrees of Kevin Bacon" (the famous game in which every actor can be linked back, film by film, to the actor Kevin Bacon). But there are simple scaffolds available that help teachers and students who are less adept at making these kinds of connections. For example, there is the AlphaBoxes template which is simply a chart with a box for each letter of the alphabet. The student is encouraged to come up with a text beginning with the letter a, and the letter b, and so on, all related to some central text or theme. Another classic brainstorming activity is called List/Group/Label (Taba, 1967) in which students are given a topic and then must brainstorm as many words that can be thought of related to that topic. For purposes of assembling text sets, this activity can be adapted so that students are challenged to think of texts that are similar or have a similar theme. The second part of this activity is a good fit for the second stage of curation—Organizing. During this step, students are challenged to group all the texts they have come up with and then label these groups. This kind of activity can help students realize they actually are coming from funds of knowledge (Gonzalez et al., 2005) about whatever is being discussed and they are capable of making connections between texts themselves without having to be spoon-fed by the teacher.

I have found word lists (and word webbing) to be powerful tools for helping students build text sets. Sometimes growing out of the words generated during the List/Group/Label activity, these lists can lead students to make connections between different texts or different elements of texts.

> ### DICTIONARY OF SLANG
>
> Compile a dictionary of slang words that you have encountered in the past or are encountering now. Please keep this list PG-rated. Simply list the slang word on the left of the page, and then provide your own definition of the slang word on the right of the page. You may want to divide your dictionary into categories of words, such as "old" and "current" words, and/or words related to work and/or words from various localities where you have lived or even slang words/phrases that you only use within your family. You will also be asked to reflect on the potential meaning of this assignment for middle school or high school students.
>
> Have you provided clear definitions for each of the words?
> Have you categorized groups of words (when appropriate) in a
>   meaningful way?

Sometimes just asking kids to collect words can help them see links. One assignment I have done over the years is to assign students to compile a Dictionary of Slang.

Of course, this kind of focus on language in the Collecting stage can bleed over into the Organizing stage, as we start to discuss the different Discourse and discourse communities we all belong to (Gee, 1996). A Primary Discourse encompasses social practices related to such groups as family, race, ethnicity, religion, while discourse with a small "d" relates to our everyday use of language (Trier, 2006). Just asking kids to think about the words they use in different Discourse communities (and how those words show up in texts) can be a powerful organizer for a developing text set.

Sometimes, as a simple scaffold, I suggest pairings of songs with poems. For example, Bruno Mars's "Just the Way You Are," which praises the beauty of a woman, can be paired with "She Walks in Beauty" by Lord Byron. Or Natalie Merchant's "Where I Go," in which she sings about wandering through nature to soothe her mind, could be paired with Wordsworth's "I Wander Lonely as a Cloud." I'm careful not to always go from the pop song to the canonical poem, or else it just becomes the "spoonful of sugar." We sometimes go from canonical to pop and then back again. It can become a kind of game that is a welcome alternative to some "bell work" worksheet. Creating these kinds of pairings can become addicting. And they can build in length and span so that they soon must reside in a Word document or in a PowerPoint or Slides presentation given to the entire class. The text set isn't thrown away at the end of the "unit," but becomes part of the curation process that underlies each student's learning experience for the entire year or for several years.

Learning Logs

One important part of the Collecting stage is that students keep some kind of learning log. Learning logs have long been suggested as beneficial to students for many reasons, as a learning-to-learn tool, as a memory aid, as method of reflection and thinking (Vacca et al., 2020), but I rarely see them used as an ongoing chronicle of student learning. And yet students with smartphones are walking around with all the tools they need for creating complete multimodal learning logs. An important part of the Collecting stage is just documenting what has been read and viewed. Students should be expected to keep an ongoing chronicle of their learning. Of course, this log can be on paper if desired, but I usually encourage students to keep digital learning logs, complete with embedded hyperlinks to sites that relate to whatever is being collected.

Embedding hyperlinks into learning logs (and whatever students are writing) is a great way to help kids make connections to what they are reading and viewing and to look at overarching themes and their reactions. Keeping a learning log preserves the experiential side of arts-based learning, instantly allowing the student to compare and contrast reading and viewing experiences as they take them in. Not only is using hyperlinks just a good skill to have for online writing, it forces students to make links, so to speak, within their own minds. If the student is required to embed links in their writing, then there is the necessity to think outside of the text that is being read or written. It allows students to comment on something they are saying, forcing them to sit outside of the text, as a critic would do.

A great way to teach the concept of hyperlinking is to show video clips from the old series *Mystery Science Theater* or *Pop-Up Videos*. In both of these shows, comic asides delivered by actors or in print model what hyperlinking can be. Students might not realize that this kind of commenting is permitted when they are reading or viewing texts at school. They are used to texts being taught as monolithic messages, with no real input from the reader. Getting students used to being critics requires them to exercise some different muscles and may take time. Students are used to years and years of attempting to produce the correct answer. Becoming their own readers and writers and critics is not going to happen overnight. Early on, when I'm working with students, I require a minimum number of hyperlinks in their learning logs. But, after several weeks pass by, I notice that I don't have to insist upon hyperlinking—it becomes a part of their digital journaling and writing. In fact, sometimes I have to suggest to certain students that they cut back on the hyperlinking, because they are inserting hyperlinks into almost every sentence. This can lead to an interesting whole-class discussion about when to hyperlink, qualities of effective hyperlinks, and how to know when there are too many hyperlinks.

Summing up the Collecting stage, Ms. Davis and Mrs. Haynes together describe their focus on text sets. "This building of text sets ended up spanning our entire English Department. As we dug into *The Hate U Give*, classroom discussions revolved around important topics from the novel: police brutality, character analysis, racism, transformation (coming of age) and finding one's voice. The discussion immediately showed the level of impact the book made on the students through the various perspectives and personal connections students shared. For example, students talked about their own interactions with police officers, discussing how to handle traffic stops similar to those in the novel. The students reached a consensus that it's best to comply with officer orders, but also to record the interaction in case things took a negative turn. It was evident that students saw themselves in the same shoes as the character Khalil, who is killed by a policeman in one of the opening chapters of the book, and that they wanted to protect themselves from his fate. We continued to build layer upon layer of texts related to the themes of *The Hate U Give*. Growing up in Mississippi, Angie Thomas was inspired by the rapper Tupac Shakur. In various interviews, Thomas shares that she would always listen and analyze his lyrics. The 'Thug Life' tattoo Shakur had on his body was his way of constantly speaking out about society's hate to infants. Tupac is shown discussing this acronym in a clip available on YouTube (https://youtu.be/QCEf557fNYg; HIP HOP CLASSIC, 2010) in which he explains the acronym, saying that "The Hate U Give little infants fucks everybody." Thomas was able to use that acronym in her fictional community of "Garden Heights," where *The Hate U Give* is set. *The Hate U Give* was her vision, letting everyone know that there are issues we need to discuss in our communities to make them better places for children so that they can live safely and thrive. We had our students explore Shakur's lyrics by reading excerpts from Shakur's anthology of lyrics and poetry *The Rose that Grew from Concrete* (Shakur, 2009).

"Both during the reading of *The Hate U Give* and after the class had finished the novel, the students were assigned to read other texts that featured characters who needed to speak out. For example, the students read the short story 'The Lottery' by Shirley Jackson (Jackson, 1949). They also watched a film adaptation of the story (Encyclopedia Britannica, 1969/2019). Jackson's classic plot is set in a small town that allows a deadly, annual tradition in which one community member is stoned to death. The tradition was allowed to continue because no one in the community had spoken out against it. Both *The Hate U Give* and 'The Lottery' deal with the theme of the importance of speaking up, using one's voice.

"The novel *Speak* (Anderson, 1999/2019) was also assigned for many related reasons. At the beginning of the novel, the main character's voice was taken due to an abusive incident she experiences over the summer before high school. As students listened to the audio version of the novel, they were able to have continuing, deep discussions about speaking up for themselves in positive ways. After we completed the novel, the students were asked to write an essay on the importance of using one's voice. These assignments clearly began to have a cumulative effect on the students. They began to be able to use their own experiences of times they wanted to use their voices, but felt their voices did not matter.

"We did not ignore nonfiction texts as we continued to collect. In *The Hate U Give*, the book's protagonist, Starr Carter, evolved into an activist at the end of the book realizing the power of her voice. Many of our students had participated in the national walk-out day in the spring of 2018, protesting gun violence in schools. This example of student activism was fresh in their memories, so we shared further examples of activism with them. In groups, students researched athletes who used their status to fight for justice. In these groups, students took on assigned roles: facilitator, reporter, recorder, but all had to do some research. The athletes to be researched included Muhammad Ali, Serena Williams, Tommie Smith, John Carlos, Colin Kaepernick, and LeBron James. Groups were instructed to research these athletes' causes, use of voice as protest and the cost they may have paid for their activism. During the sharing out, groups spoke out about how these men and women inspired them to fight for justice even in the face of consequences."

As mentioned earlier, the moment when Ms. Davis told students to take out their phones and to start researching athletes led to the writing of this book. I realized that I was witnessing a teacher and students who were in the process of curating their literacy lives. This chapter has focused on all the ways that students and teachers can take those first steps of curation, becoming collectors using their phones or via tablets or via scanning hard

---

GUIDING QUESTIONS FOR THE COLLECTING STAGE

What has been the most memorable text you have read, viewed, or listened to in the last week? In the last month? In the last year?
Choose one of these and try to describe why it affected you—what, specifically, did the author do that moved you?
Has your ability to see and hear and read deeply changed? If so, how?
Have you enlarged your capacity to see and hear?
Are you noticing things differently than you have in the past? If so, what?
Name one detail that you've noticed in some text that you've been reading or viewing. Why do you think you noticed it?
What text(s) has moved you to search out other texts? If so, what?
How have your eyes been opened by what you've been collecting?

copies. Many of these Collecting activities have a high "fun" factor. Saying that the Collecting stage is playful, however, shouldn't imply that the texts being read and written are necessarily fun. *The Hate U Give* is a powerful, often depressing text that led the Glenville students to make many connections that might have been fun to make but which also helped them to grow and develop their literacy lives, especially in light of current events. The early Collecting activities described in this chapter set us and our students up for activities that take us and our students more deeply into curating their own learning. In the next chapter, the focus will be Organizing one's collection. One of the first assignments I often give to help students thinking about organizing involves building a text set around everyone's favorite topic—ourselves.

CHAPTER 3

Organizing

The second step involves being able to see patterns (or not) in what has been collected. This step involves categorization, of course, but also creativity in seeing how ideas, concepts, and objects can be organized in new ways, using new schemata. This Organizing step also demands that each student think about the methods of organization that are best for them. What devices and platforms are available and preferred? What naming system makes past collecting accessible, even across disciplines?

Now that a foundation of Collecting has been set in place, how do we help students organize their collections? How do they begin to become true curators of their learning? What are some different patterns of classification that humans have used across time? And what are the technical affordances (New London Group, 1996) that might influence the way we organize and keep track of all that we collect digitally? The process of discussing with students the many issues surrounding the organizing of artifacts could become a worthwhile educational endeavor in itself, helping kids to think about their own learning (Palincsar & Brown, 1984).

As all of us continue to refine our collections, we must pay attention to the ways that technical tools are constantly changing. How can we make sure that we are preserving artifacts in ways that they can be seen and enjoyed across platforms and using different devices? What are the tools that all curators must be knowledgeable about, and how can we keep updated on those tools? We need to help students become connoisseurs not only of texts they are collecting, but also of the platforms and formats that are being used to house and "publish" these collections.

There is no doubt that the technology can get labor-intensive! Maintaining digital collections might seem to be less work than physical ones that have to be carried and shelved and dusted and conserved, but how many of us have had the experience of organizing our musical playlists on one platform (iTunes, for example) only to make the shift to Spotify or Pandora? Or moving from one platform or system to the next, or indeed of digitizing older materials and applying metadata to it all. Those who collect artifacts don't have to worry about this particular kind of impermanence.

A few years ago, one of my colleagues showed me an elaborate vinyl collection in which he had pieces of paper with extensive notes Scotch-taped to the album covers. I'm not sure, but I doubt that he digitized those album notes, meaning that anyone who wanted to access his notes had to have physical possession of the album and its cover. Similarly, I was recently at a university library archive and saw the preserved scrapbooks from a local theater. These scrapbooks contained amazing documents—photos, press clippings, and notes that the actors and directors had written. Unfortunately, none of it has been digitized. These items are only preserved in huge, unwieldy scrapbooks (about four feet by four feet in size). The items on each page are glued to the page, with multiple items on each page. Unfortunately, the only way that a person could have access to this material would be to go to the university archive and perhaps take a picture of the page that had the desired document. I know that my method of organizing my personal photos has changed many times over the decades, from making a lot of prints and putting them in photo albums to digitizing the photo files and organizing them by month and year on my laptop. I want to have access to my photos and be able to find them without having to go through a stack of photo albums or a four-by-four scrapbook!

In essence, this crucial Organizing stage of the curation process is not only about looking for patterns in texts, but also having a conversation about the mechanics of organizing—how do we organize the texts that are meaningful to us, and how do we do that in a way that is useful to us and leads, perhaps, to the next stage of the curation process—repurposing or creating? Are we going to be able to access what we've collected in the future, or will it be such a disorganized mess that it is difficult, if not impossible, to find anything that we need?

And it's worth pointing out to students that there is no one right answer for how to organize. This can frustrate teachers who tend to like having assignments turned in according to prescribed formats. But if the curation process is going to survive and thrive outside of school for kids, we have to let them at least somewhat develop their own organizational patterns and use of available platforms. Even apart from the changing technology, each person has different preferences about how to categorize various texts so that they are meaningfully and easily accessible. In this chapter, I'm going to describe some assignments that the Glenville teachers and I have used over the years to get the students thinking about different ways to organize the texts they are collecting, even as they move toward the Repurposing stage. These assignments are often open and not rigid in format.

It is during this Organizing step that students begin to learn that the curation model is, indeed, an individual journey, and a recursive one. When it's done right, the curation process is constantly ongoing, as long as students are curious about what is next and how they can move forward and back into the collecting step. A main focus of this chapter is the description of the creation of online spaces for organizing texts and of digital portfolios that allow students to continuously reflect on their work, including an assessment and self-assessment component. Each student's space—starting with the Multimodal Memoir project described below—becomes the home base for assessment of curriculum objectives and for ongoing curation, with the goal of truly blurring the lines between in-school learning and out-of-school learning.

THINKING ABOUT YOUR LEARNING
MANAGEMENT SYSTEM (LMS)

Most districts provide access to some learning management system (LMS) that allows for storage and retrieval of student work. At Glenville, teachers were supposed to use either Schoology or Google Classroom. Other commonly used LMSs are Blackboard, Moodle, and Edmodo. Most LMSs include some kind of space for storing stuff. Teachers who are in districts that use Google Classroom, for example, can have their students set up a very simple space using Google Sites. This would be important when working in Google Classroom, or student work will be lost to the "stream" that is Google Classroom postings. In Google Classroom, if one wants to find a post from a few weeks or even a few days ago, one has to scroll back up through the stream. The Glenville teachers use Schoology to house student assignments and assessments. Teachers who are not happy with the official LMS can still set up wikis for their classes using free sites such as PBWorks (pbworks.com), setting up a space for storing any documents needed by the class, from readings and videos to student exhibitions.

MULTIMODAL MEMOIR

But, regardless of LMS, how should teachers start the conversation about organizing? I usually begin by having a conversation about all the texts that have influenced me and entertained me over the years. I do this in the context of an assignment that I call the Multimodal Memoir. Students will soon be doing their own memoirs, so I start by exhibiting my memoir. This is an assignment that I've written about (Batchelor et al., 2015; Kist, 2010, 2017) and that continues to be powerful for kids of all ages. It helps move students from the Collecting stage to the Organization stage of curation.

The Multimodal Memoir asks students to think about all the texts that have made a major impact on their lives. This part of the assignment involves Collecting. The next part of the assignment asks them to think about major themes of these influences. This part of the assignment involves Organization. The assignment asks students to look at trends—what kinds of texts have made an impact? Are their certain forms of representation that have made more of a difference than others? The assignment is motivating in that students are performing this kind of organization and trend analysis regarding most people's favorite subject—themselves.

I have built up my memoir over the years in PowerPoint and then converted over to Google Slides. In my memoir, I include quite a variety of texts that have been influential in my life—songs, movies, books, and visual art. I also talk about the ways that I consume and organize the texts that I read and view. I mostly have my memoir organized in chronological order, but I point out that there are many other ways to organize one's Multimodal Memoir.

After I've shown my memoir, we have an open discussion about all the many kinds of texts that we consume. One of the key characteristics of digital media that makes thinking about curation necessary is the sheer volume of texts that we consume. It's usually very easy to get classroom consensus that we are all swamped with texts. No longer bound to watching just three television channels or reading what we find at the corner newsstand or listening to what we find at the record store, we (kids and adults alike) enjoy a wide variety of text types that often span the globe. Students now have the capability of accessing Japanese anime or the latest hip-hop anthem, or the latest YA series book, all on phones they carry in their pockets. During these early memoir discussions, I find that most of my students have amazingly eclectic tastes, ranging from the music of Frank Sinatra and Run DMC to the art of Andy Warhol to the adventures of Anne of Green Gables. These are only a fraction of the artists and characters and texts that spill out as we talk about the texts of our lives.

I started doing this assignment years ago with the goal of helping students to realize that their interests have value regardless of favored form of representation, and that their fandom has value. As I thought more about the curation model, I felt that the Multimodal Memoir served as a strong foundational assignment, demonstrating that students are already collectors, and that they already have a developed aesthetic sense (van Leeuwen, 2018). If done at the beginning of the year, this assignment can become the baseline text set, the primary collection that the student may return to and revise throughout the year. But why stop with one year? Students could routinely revisit their memoirs throughout their entire schooling. Educators can have meaningful conversations with students about criteria for deciding what is useful and desirable and enjoyable to collect. This emerging criteria list should be fluid and often revisited not only by individual students, but also at the classroom and school levels. The joy in collecting should be promoted as a cross-discipline phenomenon, so that students become adept at finding and collecting texts no matter what the content area.

This assignment asks students to begin to collect and narrate their own literacy lives as experienced via the plethora of texts they have encountered over a lifetime of "reading" and "writing." This seemingly simple task goes beyond just collecting pictures and poems and songs from one's earliest years. The Multimodal Memoir asks students to synthesize and write about these texts in ways that push them to find the threads between them, the connecting threads that carry unique meaning and resonance for them as learners, readers, and writers. As I began to research and describe new literacies, one of the most powerful examples I found was Tom Romano's "multigenre paper" idea (Romano, 2000). Romano's idea was to allow students to write the traditional research paper using different genres—from an obituary to a menu to a classified ad. Students would have to do just as much research on whatever topic or era was being researched, but the form of the product would be multigenre and/or multimodal.

Over the years, I added this multigenre element to a typical "literacy autobiography" assignment in which students are asked to write about their reading and writing lives. What I now call the Multimodal Memoir assignment has been seen to be successful both with really little kids (Batchelor et al., 2015) as well as with pre-service professionals (Kist, 2017; Meixner et al., 2018). The introduction to the assignment follows; for the full assignment sheet as I hand it out, see the Appendix.

As with the text set assignment described in the previous chapter, students can assemble their memoirs as a Word document or a PowerPoint or Slides presentation. Students who are skilled at video editing might make their memoir into a video documentary. Or students may use other platforms such as VoiceThread or Comic Life. I do not put many parameters on the assignment format. I do generally schedule one or two class periods in which students present their memoirs to the entire class and there are time limits set for that part of the assignment.

This assignment allows students to riff on all of the many texts that coalesce around a theme or topic. Students also get a chance to practice their aesthetic skills and apply them to the chronicle of their own textual lives, moving them and the entire class to a more biographical-driven approach (Herrera, 2016; Muhammad, 2020).

I think what has impressed and surprised me over the years of doing this project is the depth of the texts represented in the memoirs. And I have been impressed with the themes—how integral family members are to literacy and how often there is one special teacher or librarian mentioned. I have done this assignment with kids as young as 1st grade (Batchelor et al., 2015) and been similarly impressed with the texts they talk about from their 6-year-old lives. With little kids, we start with autobiographical picture books *David Gets His Drum* (Francis et al., 2002), *Through My Eyes* (Bridges & Lundell, 1999), and *The Art of Miss Chew* (Polacco, 2012). We give them a

> ### MULTIMODAL MEMOIR ASSIGNMENT
>
> This assignment encourages you to think about all the various texts of your life as they relate to reading and writing. Your own history as a reader, writer, and viewer of texts will have a significant impact on your future literacy experiences. Doing the following exercise should help you reflect on your own multimodal textual past.
>
> Your objective is to create a screen-based representation of the influence of these various texts on your life from childhood to today. Such texts may include books, films, television shows, music, newspapers, magazines, sports, restaurants, food, cars, fashion, architecture, and/or interior design (to name a few examples.) Visit Google Images, Flickr, Yahoo Image Search, YouTube, etc., and find some images or video clips related to the important texts of your life. You might want to start with the book you shared during your video introduction and then riff off of that.
>
> You may create this assignment in any one of the following programs: VoiceThread (http://voicethread.com); PowerPoint; Prezi (prezi.com); or digital storytelling tools such as Storymaker (https://www.story-maker .org/), Umajin (http://www.umajin.com/), or MixBook (http://www .mixbook.com); or create a comic book portrayal of a character or yourself using Comic Life (http://plasq.com/comiclife). Audio may be recorded using Audacity or some other recording software. You will need to create your memoir in such a way that it can be uploaded to our learning space.

brainstorming worksheet called "Who Am I?" that gets them thinking about the various facets of their lives, such as favorite music, sports, books, and games (see Batchelor et al., 2015). Then we show them how to copy/paste images or video or sound files into a Google Slides presentation, and they are off!

One of the most important items on the assignment checklist relates to the Organizing stage of the curation process. I try to challenge students to think about themes they see in the texts that have been important to them. This item in the checklist reads: "Does your autobiography appear to have been just thrown together at the last minute, or has some real thought gone into it? Are there some themes and/or storylines that thread throughout your autobiography?" With this assignment, we begin to have our first discussions about how we organize the stuff we collect—chronologically? By theme? By form? By level of impact? By physical attractiveness?

Once there is acknowledgment of the need to organize, the next step is to think about *how* to organize, and this involves some level of criticism; students need to begin to examine texts critically and intertextually. The Memoir assignment requires students to contextualize the texts of their lives both in terms of their own trajectories, but also in terms of the lives of the creators of these texts and the lives of other audience members for these texts, including some of their own family members. Although the original intent of the Multimodal Memoir assignment was to get students simply to take notice of the variety of modes we consume, it seems like the assignment has gotten bigger. In the early days of my doing the assignment, students would bring in their PowerPoints on jump drives. We would plug them into the classroom computer and wait for them to load. They were powerful, even then. Now, students come in with Google Slides with embedded video clips, some of which they have written and directed themselves, or they have used Comic Life to create a comic book of their own lives. Or they have used VoiceThread to poignantly comment on a key text that was introduced to them by a grandmother or uncle. The assignment's purpose seems to have morphed and broadened over the years until it has become at the core of curating—it's a vehicle for getting started organizing and doing so with the texts that are most important to each of us. It is, essentially, the first step in a kind of cross-disciplinary curation of a literacy life, allowing for some critical literacy practice and a true blurring of intra-school boundaries and boundaries between school and the outside world.

Of course, as mentioned in the previous chapter, the roots of critical literacy lie in the work of Freire (1970/2000) who claimed literacy as having the ability to set free both the oppressed and the oppressor (both of whom are oppressed, according to Freire). People need to learn to "read the world" (Freire & Macedo, 1987). Unfortunately, Street's (1995) depiction of an autonomous (top-down) view of literacy in which there is one right way to read and write still seems to be dominant in public education in North America. Describing the ideal of critical literacy, Luke and Woods (2009) wrote, "Readers and writers use a variety of modes of inscription—print, oral, and multimedia—to understand, analyze, critique, and transform their social, cultural, and political worlds" (p. 9). Similarly, Morrell et al. (2013) wrote, "Students who desire social justice must be critical consumers and producers of texts across multiple genres of both traditional and new media" (p. 5).

Of course, there have been many projects written about over the years that describe classroom projects involving critical media literacy, including having kids look critically at magazines and films (Skinner, 2007), memes (Crovitz & Moran, 2020), school newsmagazines (Heffernan et al., 2020), sports coverage (Rodesiler, 2019), and superhero films (Toliver, 2017). Other research projects have asked students to create theater pieces (Rozansky & Aagesen, 2010) and autoethnography (Camangian, 2010). Examples come from a broad array of settings including ELL classrooms (Choudhury & Share, 2012) and makerspaces (Assaf et al., 2021).

Being critically literate does involve some level of *metaconsciousness* (Luke & Woods, 2009). It's helpful to talk with students about what they are thinking and give them practice in "being meta"—thinking about thinking. I have found the Memoir assignment, perhaps because it does let them think and write about themselves, has been a good first step.

Ga-Vita Haynes described an assignment that she has used at Glenville, especially during the pandemic, that also helped jumpstart some theme-building. It's called "What's in Your Head?" "We had the feeling on Zoom that many times, when discussions arise, students would be shy to speak. They might not want to participate in the discussions because of anger, frustration, or managing their depression. Or they just were too tired due to working long hours the night before. After observing these tendencies, we wanted to create a way for students to help understand what they might be thinking at that moment in time.

"We thought of letting the students answer the question 'What's in your head?' The students were able to discuss the question first. Then we had them each create a silhouette of a person's head. The students had two options. The first option was to draw a head on a white piece of paper and the second option was to use search and find a coloring page on Google of the figure of a head and save it as a PDF. I immediately started modeling the exercise for students, finding my own head silhouette. I used my Cricut machine to cut a head silhouette and began using cut-out magazine pictures to help me with the inside, filling my head silhouette. The assignment was to use pictures or words to describe what the student was thinking about at that time. We wanted the students to try to get a grasp of what they were carrying with them in their heads. Some students asked many questions. They wanted to know if they were allowed to put something negative inside the head silhouette. In addition, the students wanted to know if they could draw the pictures instead of trying to find some in magazines. We did not realize that some students did not have magazines at home or a printer to print a head silhouette to even get started, so there was some frustration at the beginning of the activity.

"By the end, products were personalized and informative. We, as educators, were able to understand what each student was thinking at that moment, with pictures they had drawn, words they simply wrote, and pictures they found. After the students completed the assignment, they were able to share, if they wanted to, and then upload a picture to the class Schoology page. If the students did not want to upload via Schoology, they were able to send a picture to one of us and then we would upload into Schoology so the student would be able to receive credit for the assignment.

"This assignment taught the students to understand what they are thinking in that moment with pictures, words, and drawings. They reflected on the fact that in order to find your voice, you need to understand your thoughts to formulate the words/thoughts to support your thinking process. The students gained so much from this assignment, strategies they can use when having discussions in class or just trying to solve a problem. The students now understand to think first before speaking, to gather one's thoughts for a better overall outcome."

Doing a quickwrite (described below) can help kids process what they are thinking and what themes they see arising within the texts they are reading and viewing. Quickwrites can serve as a writing-to-learn activity by providing students with an opportunity to recall, clarify, critically question, and organize the texts being read and viewed. Throwing out a critical question or prompt occasionally can help students begin to see patterns. It's important not to let these quickwrites be throwaways, however. They can be used as exit slips to assist the teacher's assessment of the class, but it should be emphasized to students that these quickwrites are for their own benefit, to perhaps include in their Learning Logs and to help them begin to organize their curations.

Over the years, I have had students ask me if it's okay for them to draw their quickwrites, and of course I say yes. Being in a digital environment helps enormously in this regard, both in terms of allowing students to use all kinds of media in their quickwrites, and also to preserve the quickwrites within their multimodal learning logs.

Quickwrites (Due During Various Class Periods)

A prompt will be given related to a particular topic on designated days and you will be given a time limit to respond. These quickwrites should be submitted for credit, but a copy of each quickwrite should be kept and added to your Learning Log.

Criteria

Reflection of Course Content/Application in the Entries (35 points)

Are you reacting to specific quotes (include page numbers or link) from the texts?
Is there evidence that you have spent time with each text?
Are you organizing the texts in a meaningful way?
Are your ideas explained in such a way that they are understandable?

Mechanics (15 points)

Are there typos and/or standard English mechanics errors in the writing?

Once we have established a pattern in the class for valuing multiple forms of representation, by doing the Multimodal Memoir and What's in Your Head? activities, I try to make the transition to having students become more vocally critical, to make assertions about a text, and to do so in such a way that is defensible. I have found that a relatively smooth way to make this transition is to assign students to review a film. Using criteria adapted from Costanzo (2008), I ask students to look at a film's point of view and the context in which it was made. Who is the intended audience for this film? I ask the student to state their own personal opinion, from an aesthetic perspective—is this a film you enjoyed? Just so that there is some guidance for students wondering what film to choose, I often suggest a film be chosen related to a theme we have been discussing in class. However, I am open to suggestion from students regarding what film they review. Again, as in the close-reading exercises described in the previous chapter, I have found that students are more adept at reviewing films than they are at reviewing novels or short stories.

FILM REVIEW

Write a 3- to 5-page (double-spaced, 12-point font) review of a film that focuses on [a theme we have been working on].

Criteria

Have you chosen a film that relates to our theme and explained how it does (via a plot summary)? Have you also described what the film's point of view seems to be about our theme? Also, describe what group (age group, gender, ethnic group, or socioeconomic status) this film is designed to appeal to. (25 points)

How does the film use filmmaking techniques to make its point (camera movement, editing, use of music and sound effects, acting)? (10 points)

What is your opinion about the film's effectiveness? How effectively does it achieve its purpose? What can you say about the format, structure, and style that make it particularly effective or ineffective? Did you find yourself resisting or going toward the film's messages? (25 points)

Is your review well organized and clear (easy to follow)? (20 points)

Have you paid attention to the length requirement and to using Standard English, including spelling, punctuation, mechanics, documentation, and format? (20 points)

Adapted from Costanzo (2008).

PORTFOLIOS

Now that a few assignments have been accumulated and some discussion about organization has been accomplished, it's time to talk about organizing the collection as a whole. Following along with curation's arts-based theme, it makes sense to ask students to set up portfolios for themselves. Indeed, the class should set up its organizers, using one or more of the platforms mentioned above, quite close to the beginning of the semester, so that we are never faced with disorganization and the need to spend valuable time going back through all our bits and pieces. Setting up a receptacle, an organizer, for curation is actually necessary toward the beginning of the school year or the semester so that we don't lose a minute of our collecting and organizing! We don't want to wait until half the year is over to figure out what to do with all of our stuff!

Artists of all kinds put together portfolios of their work. In my early years of teaching, I would have students create writing portfolios on paper that I would keep in my classroom. Despite our best efforts, however, it seemed that the stack of portfolios didn't seem to be able to be carried down the hall to the next grade teacher. They would languish on a shelf, with the next year's teacher not really knowing what to do with them. Now that we can have digital portfolios, some literacy scholars have advocated for their use due to convenience and mobility that we did not have in a pre-computer era. These digital portfolios are seen as providing affordances for reflection and creative thinking while also making learning public (Autrey et al., 2007; Fahey et al., 2007) in a way difficult to imagine in a paper-based era.

In the literacy field, it's probably true that we have thought of portfolios more in terms of composition assessment than we have in terms of the arts. Dating back to the early scholars of composition studies (Emig, 1971; Flower & Hayes, 1977) we've been focused on getting students to understand "the writing process." Building on the work of Donald Graves (1983/2003), Nancie Atwell designed a portfolio-based approach to both writing and reading instruction (Atwell, 2015). I have drawn heavily on her model as I have assigned my students to set up their own portfolios for curation purposes. Again, I don't put many demands on students regarding format. I allow them to set up a Google Site or just a Google Doc containing all of the elements. I have had students keep portfolios within PowerPoint with embedded hyperlinks or even a wiki. I'm looking more for the elements— how have they organized what they have collected? Students are not evaluated on how "pretty" their portfolios are or how technically sophisticated.

At this point, even early in the curation process, I expect students to have a fairly vibrant collection of texts with evidence of quantity, variety, quality, and frequency of contribution to the collection. They should, of course, include their Multimodal Memoirs as well as other text sets they have created according to themes we have been studying. In the portfolio, I should get a sense that students have been reading and viewing widely. There should be evidence that students have gone beyond readings and viewings we have done in class and brought in texts they have encountered in their lives outside school. And, of course, there should be evidence of pop culture. I usually add to the portfolio checklist some expectation of "pleasure" reading and viewing—a certain number of hours per week. And, yes, I do count reading on screens as reading, although I usually say that reading and writing of social media don't count for this assignment. I want students to look at pieces of art that have been created intentionally by someone, not spend time participating in a social media conversation.

I usually ask for an introduction to the portfolio in which the student is to talk about what Atwell calls "reading and writing territories." What are the typical kinds of texts that are being read and viewed? How have these texts intersected (or not) with the themed readings and viewings we have been doing in class?

As far as the body of the portfolio, I expect to see a certain number of text sets related to whatever theme we are working on in class. In Ms. Davis's case, the students had collected examples of both nonfiction and fiction characters speaking out—from real-life athletes protesting injustices to fictional characters such as Starr Carter's involvement in protests within the book *The Hate U Give*. She also spent time looking at characters who did not speak out, such as the townspeople in "The Lottery."

One of the simple extensions I have done at this stage of Organizing is to assign each student to add one poem or song lyric to their text set. I usually say "Just one" and end up getting many more. I sometimes put up a large piece of chart paper on a bulletin board or whiteboard and create a graffiti wall on which students can write quotes or entire lyrics that have moved them.

GUIDING QUESTIONS FOR THE ORGANIZING STAGE

Write a reflective letter describing what this assignment has meant to you. Have you grown as a reader? If not, why not? What now? What are some themes that you are seeing in your reading? What are some texts that you want to keep and, perhaps, re-read? What are some goals you have for your reading in the future?

What themes did you start with and what themes did you end with? Explain how they morphed.

What has your learning log revealed to you about directions you might want to take during the Repurposing stage?

As we move toward the Repurposing stage, I want to see that the student has paid attention to their Learning Log. The contents of the Log can sometimes point the way toward the creations that the students will want to do when we move into Repurposing. A guiding question that I ask is: "What themes did you start with and what themes did you end with? Explain how they morphed." And then, finally, pointing the way to the next stage, I usually ask students something like, "What do you want to create now?" I want to get a sense of this without laying on too much in the way of assignment expectations. "Now that we've been thinking about this theme in our collecting and organizing, what next? Is there something you would like to write or correct?" Some possibilities for the Repurposing stage will be suggested in the next chapter.

CHAPTER 4

Repurposing

This third step involves transforming what has been collected into a new whole, most probably exhibited or performed for an audience (but the audience could simply be the student). How has the collecting and organizing suggested something new, either in terms of concept or presentation? How can the collecting and organizing be structured to form narratives and other kinds of exhibitions that serve to represent individual inquiry paths? How do the forms of representation used during the repurposing help us develop new ways of knowing?

Once students have experienced a variety of texts and developed a rich and organized collection, how can we help them think about and repurpose some of their various artifacts into something new? How can we help students draw upon their collections to formalize their own inquiry paths?

This chapter outlines the Repurposing stage in which students take the collection of texts that they have assembled and demonstrate how this collection may be repurposed into some new creation. The curation model embraces a variety of types of media texts. This chapter will focus on how the Glenville teachers used photography—both still photos and moving pictures—during the repurposing stage. As previously described, Glenville students had already been steeped in viewing films together, both in class and at the cinema. They seemed more than ready to think about using their cameras for their own purposes.

Within this stage, there is usually some kind of presentation of the new work, either online or in person. How do students present their inquiry journeys using multiple forms of representation, and, in the process of doing so, create innovative new texts? What are the best ways for students to show off their collections? Which pieces should be foregrounded? Which pieces should go into "storage" for a bit? The presentations that occur as culminating events could follow principles of thematic learning, as students feature certain pieces according to the "season" (Jacobs, 1989). These presentations can then take each student back to the collecting stage, as each is potentially inspired not only by their own presentation but also those of others, demonstrating the true recursive nature of the curation process.

What happens during this stage often involves some kind of *remix*. "The term remix refers to the use, combination, and manipulation of cultural artifacts to create something new (Knobel & Lankshear, 2008; Rust & Ballard, 2016) and was most commonly associated with music until recently . . . At present, remix has come to be seen as a form of meaning making that extends beyond music and includes many other creative endeavors" (Gainer & Lapp, 2010a, pp. 17–18). "In all cases, the classroom remix led to a blend of patterns and hierarchies that led the teachers, students, and researchers to challenge assumptions and raise new questions about how language-arts classrooms function in the digital age" (Callahan & King, 2011, pp. 134–135). I believe that the use of the word "remix" is analogous to the Repurposing stage of the curation model—in this stage, students get to "mix and match" some or all of the texts they have collected, putting them together in new ways.

My work at Glenville also led me to see the value of thinking about *place-based literacies*. The history of Glenville and its present victories and challenges seemed to be woven into the repurposings that I saw students creating. During the ELA team weekly discussions, the place we were in—the neighborhood and school of Glenville—was a significant player in the work of the teachers and students. The students were writing and experiencing texts through the lenses of their experiences, and, for most of them, those experiences were linked tightly to Glenville as a place. Of course, this is not surprising to any literacy scholar who is familiar with the New Literacy Studies (NLS) perspective. For NLS researchers, literacy is deeply bound up in the everyday locations of people's lives (Barton & Hamilton, 1998; Gee, 1996; Street, 1995). To look at people's literacies devoid of their contexts is impossible. There have been many recent studies that have looked at place in the literacy classroom—within the context of digital storytelling, for example (Chisholm & Trent, 2013), or conducting oral histories with community members (Hadley, 2019), and just as a means to improving writing, multimodal or otherwise (Esposito, 2012; Stanton & Sutton, 2012). Multimodal storytelling has been used to help youths on both sides of the border between Mexico and the United States practice their "fugitive literacies" (Gonzales et al., 2020).

In November of 2019, I was in Ms. Davis's room as she was facilitating a discussion about the differences between the film and the book of *The Hate U Give*. "What was different between the book and the film?" she asked. In answer to a later question, almost every kid said the book was "better" than the film. Ms. Davis mentioned a crowd scene that she felt should have been in the movie. "We know there have been a lot of times when people have rioted, when they have cases like this. Do we agree with Big Mav that people shouldn't burn down their own neighborhoods? We need to do a lesson about the Glenville riots." The students got quiet as Ms. Davis went on. "A lot happened in this neighborhood. My grandmother's beauty salon was on 110th and Superior. . . . When they were burning down the buildings around it, she put a sign that said 'Soul Sister' on her beauty shop." You could see that the students were fascinated. She continued, "Think about all the stuff that goes on in a community. . . . We were still having murders in Cleveland up until the start of November. Do you all think that the older guys in the neighborhood, if they talked to the younger guys, could it help? When you go through something like that, you should help people. Like Big Mav. You should be mentoring . . . I don't know if they would listen. Do you think most people of color feel the same way Starr does? If so, that will be your claim, and then you are going to jump to your evidence and your counterclaim." In just a few minutes, Ms. Davis had transitioned from the text they were reading, to current events, back to the text, and on to the argumentative writing that they were about to do, weaving all of these texts into the new repurposing they were going to make. Ms. Davis constantly asked students to return to one of the texts (book or film) to support the opinion being stated. The students were learning both aesthetic analysis and critical literacy.

So many of the repurposings I saw at Glenville, especially one that involved a professional filmmaker and repeated location shoots in the neighborhood, were uniquely Glenville. They couldn't have been created anywhere else. But to be clear, repurposings do not have to be grand pieces of art. They can be as simple as what happens at an open mike session.

OPEN MIKE FRIDAY

Ga-Vita Haynes has used a simple yet meaningful repurposing strategy: Open Mike Friday. During Open Mike Friday, students have the opportunity to present some of their own repurposed work in the form of essays or poetry that they have written or sampled. Mrs. Haynes describes: "In *Bronx Masquerade* by Nikki Grimes (2017), one of the main characters spoke about his thoughts about writing an essay his teacher had asked him to write while the class studied poetry. Instead of the essay, the character wanted to share one of his poems that he created in front of the class. The teacher asked the student to bring it in on Friday. The student agreed and from that point other students wanted to share their poetry and raps they created. In the book, this concept opened many avenues for students to let their voices be heard. There were no rubrics, nor grading scales for this activity because the teacher wanted to use this opportunity for the students to express themselves.

"In the classroom, we adopted the same concept but with a twist. Each Friday, the students were given three topics to write on. They each had to write a 14-line poem that included three symbols. We wanted the students to have some type of guidance because we did not want to face students saying they did not know what to write about. After the students were given time to create, they each would have to stand in front of the class and recite the poem and speak about the three symbols they had used in the poem, to symbolize issues that were important to them. This was a graded assignment. At first, there was some hesitation from a few students—the ones who were shy and did not feel comfortable speaking in front of the class. We also had a few others who would not complete the assignment because they felt like they were not poets and that their creativity was not acceptable. After many conversations and observations of their peers' celebrating the creativity of others in front of the class, by the next Open Mike Friday, most of the students participated. After a few weeks, the students were able to create their own topics, which we voted on as a class, for the upcoming Open Mike Friday. Some topics we voted on included: Family Life, Relationships, Being Alone, Getting Things Done, Crazy Things Happen, Being Honest, and My Life. We conducted Open Mike Friday every week unless we were testing. Before the end of the year, all of the students presented in front of the class and created memories we will never forget."

REPURPOSING CURRENT EVENTS INTO ARGUMENT

The Glenville teachers were not shy about using current events as texts that would then guide a repurposing in the form of an essay. Shannon Davis describes, "I will start with a Do Now or survey using Kahoot or brief discussion to determine students' prior knowledge of the current event or topic. [Kahoot! (https://kahoot.it/) is an online quiz game tool that basically functions like a game show.] Once this is determined and briefly discussed, the next step is twofold: research and analysis. Individually or in groups, first the students will research the incident. The students/groups will have questions to guide them. Next, I will show a video from a reputable news outlet to further expound upon the incident. After researching and watching the video(s), I will spark a Socratic seminar-type discussion to gauge the students' reactions. The final part of the assignment will be connected to the standard(s) that are being covered in class. Due to the nature of some controversial current events, Socratic seminars are usually very insightful and meaningful as the students are passionate about their individual perspectives.

"A recent example was the story of runner Sha'Carri Richardson being disqualified from running during the 2021 Summer Olympics. Most were aware of the story due to the overwhelming media coverage. I decided to use this story to help students develop basic arguments, a unit we had just started. We reviewed the basic parts of an argument and the purpose of each component. Next, we read an *NY Times* article, 'Sha'Carri Richardson, A Track Sensation, Tests Positive for Marijuana.' We also watched a video clip of Richardson on *Good Morning America* apologizing for her actions. Now that the students had more information on the Olympic controversy, I wanted to hear feedback and we had a brief discussion. Interestingly, the students had varying perspectives on the situation, which made for a rich discussion. The class work was an opportunity for students to develop an argument outline revolving around Richardson's disqualification. Depending on the class and prior knowledge of students I make the choice if the students will complete the work individually or within a small group. If small groups will be used, I would review the roles of taskmaster, timekeeper, recorder, and researcher. The students will take a few minutes to choose roles. That day, the prompt was: 'Based on your knowledge of Sha-Carri Richardson's disqualification from the 2021 Olympics, respond to the prompts below: Do you think the laws surrounding marijuana use should be changed for future Olympic events (or athletes in general)?' An additional prompt was: 'Suppose you had a personal relationship with Richardson. What are two pieces of advice you would give to her in order to get past the Olympic controversy? Discuss your reasons.'

"Every time I've introduced current events it has been a positive experience. The students find the material relevant and at times relatable. As a result, there is usually extremely high student engagement. This leads to insightful student dialogue. Often, students find themselves following up on these stories on their own and as a class we often revisit the stories."

The Glenville teachers found that discussing current events would often lead to students collecting new material. Ms. Davis and Mrs. Haynes write, "Students would share stories they had read through social media, and we would locate local news stories about these events, providing real-life examples to prompt argumentative essays. We noticed that students started bringing in examples of video clips and tweets themselves, and these often stimulated further classroom discussion and writing. Recently, for example, a student brought in a YouTube clip by a rapper named Prince EA who created a video essay around his frustration about what he learned in school and its uselessness ('What is school for?', 2019). The student asked one of us, 'What do you think of this?' We immediately turned this question back to the student and asked, 'What do *you* think?' The ensuing conversation was deep, rich, and authentic as students made claims and counterclaims about the relative usefulness or lack of usefulness in the school curriculum they had experienced since kindergarten. The students saw the relevance and necessity of learning argumentative writing skills to make arguments in meaningful ways about authentic topics they cared about.

"Because of the experiences of Starr Carter (the protagonist of *The Hate U Give*), we also ended up segueing into discussing mental health issues such as post-traumatic stress disorder (PTSD) and survivor's guilt. This proved to be quite appropriate given the range of emotions we saw displayed by students after watching the film version. Starr Carter lost two friends to gun violence by the age of 16, and we watched how our students were vicariously experiencing what she was feeling. And, sadly, our students were not only having vicarious reactions—they had experienced trauma themselves. During the unit we reviewed the local Tamir Rice case as well as others that ended in police officers killing unarmed people. In two classes we watched footage of the Rice shooting, and it had a profound effect on the students. We suggest surveying students to find out if they have personal connections such as this or experience with violence in some way before showing news footage of violence.

"To help our students gain better understandings about mental health, we read an informational article and watched videos about PTSD. At the end of the unit, students were given various project options to choose. One option was to create a brochure on PTSD. Within the brochure, students documented its causes and effects on people and actual numbers and websites for people who needed help. Again, the experience of creating a product in this alternative form (a brochure) seemed to generate much serious conversation in class about taking care of oneself during and after times of enormous stress."

REPURPOSING TEXTS INTO A POSTER OR OTHER FORMS OF REPRESENTATION

In addition to brochures, I saw many student-created posters at Glenville Even a simple poster can serve to repurpose a collection of texts. I often saw repurposing posters hanging outside classrooms at Glenville. While reading *The Hate U Give*, students designed posters that included information they had gathered about the characters in the novel and how these characters shaped each other's lives. These posters could be quite literal, including quotes and descriptions of scenes from the novel. Or they could be quite abstract, with bright colors and nondescript shapes, apparently indicating plot points or emotions that those plot points evoked.

Often, it seemed that students had added their own prior knowledge of events similar to those depicted in *The Hate U Give*. Mrs. Haynes writes, "We were amazed by the way that poster creation allowed students to analyze the characters in the novel on a deeper level. . . . The poster project allowed an alternative outlet for students to process the book, and it concluded with a finished project that brought out their best work."

Of course, many teachers have encouraged students to "translate" a print text into another form of representation, whether it's a poster or a video about the book (also known as a "book trailer"), a song playlist, or a piece of visual art. I feel, however, that these tend to be one-off assignments, designed to provide extra credit rather than to truly set up a pattern of repurposing that would ultimately be woven into the curation process, showing up over the years in student portfolios.

While both the Glenville teachers and I typically will assign some kind of literary criticism and/or argumentative essay, we also make room for some alternative format Repurposing, whether it's a poster, a video, or a poem. Here is the description of such an assignment from one of my past Portfolio assignment sheets: "Please spend some time creating a work of your own choosing. The expectation is that you will do some major work repurposing the text set(s) you have collected and organized. It's possible you might continue to work on a piece that you have been working on for several months. Your new/old piece does not have to be a finished, polished work, but it does have to be some kind of Repurposing of the texts we have been collecting and organizing. Think about how you would like to grow as a curator and a creator! Ultimately, I would like you to upload not only the final draft of your piece but at least one of its earlier drafts as well."

TEACHER RESOURCE GUIDE

Another, less artistic, idea for Repurposing is to encourage students to create what I call Resource Guides. Students are challenged with this assignment to take all they have learned through Collecting and Organizing and Repurposing texts to create something that could help teachers who want to teach a certain theme or topic. The project asks students to repurpose the material using an educational lens. I form students into reading groups around particular topics or genres (urban fiction, texts focused on injustice, an issue like eating disorders); eventually the texts they collect, read, and discuss can form the basis of resource guides. The groups review and winnow down their set of texts and then present their selections to the class.

Below is the complete assignment sheet.

STILL PHOTOGRAPHY

At Glenville, Mrs. Haynes also emulated many scholars who have written about using still photography with students. As mentioned earlier, Muhammad (2020) advocates for students to be assigned to make autobiographical narratives, often resting on still pictures, as a key component

---

GENRE/AUTHOR/TOPIC RESOURCE GUIDE

For the entire semester, your small group will be immersed in the books and various texts from a chosen genre or author. You will become an expert on a genre or an author and contribute to a Resource Guide that will be of help to other students or to teachers who want to teach this genre, author, or topic. Please include the following elements.

1. Provide an introduction to your Resource Guide that identifies and describes patterns in the genre's features or author's work. What recurrent features are evident? What content is typically included? What is excluded? How are texts in the genres structured? How long is the typical text? How would you describe the writer(s) voices?
2. Collect as many examples of the genre or the works of the author or related to the topic or genre as possible. These works should all be hyperlinked to the appropriate page on Amazon.
   a) Each title should have a quick synopsis written by someone in the group. This synopsis should give at least one idea for tying the book to the Learning Standards.
   b) Each person in the group should read at least five books and be able to answer questions from the audience regarding the books read.
3. Collect as many examples of related multimodal texts as possible: video clips, websites, blogs, social media accounts (Twitter, Facebook, Instagram), lesson plans
4. Include a bullet-point list of instructional strategies and assessment ideas that could be used to teach this genre or author if you were a teacher.
5. Prepare a presentation to the class that highlights key elements of your wiki page. Make sure each group member takes part in the presentation.

---

to her historically responsive literacy framework: "Students are asked to digitally capture aspects of their communities and lives to tell a story of who they are. They may tell a story of their neighborhoods, communities, families, or any other context or cultural membership that shapes their lives and literacy practices" (p. 76).

Drawing on Wendy Ewald's work (2001), Wissman (2008) spent a year with a high school group of girls called "Sistahs" who repurposed still photography as a basis for storytelling. "In each trimester, students brought in, wrote about, and discussed personal and family photographs. As a daily ritual in the class, the sharing and discussing of these photographs helped to create a context in which images served as conduits for sharing and as the basis for storytelling. This sharing and storytelling often revolved around family members, social events, and childhood memories" (Wissman, 2008, p. 21). "Within this seemingly straightforward and uncomplicated request to bring in and share photographs, the medium of photography coupled with the act of storytelling opened up a range of possibilities for meaning making, relationship building, and learning in the classroom" (Wissman, 2008, p. 21). According to Wissman, the project allowed students to "frame their own realities" (p. 29).

Another well-documented project called "Through Students' Eyes" worked with hundreds of students over a 10-year period, asking students to take photographs and then answer questions such as "Why did you take this picture?" and "What do you like about this photograph?" (Harmon & Marquez-Zenkov, 2007; Zenkov et al., 2011). The authors of this study found that their students were grappling with some heavy issues, including economic and health concerns and violence. Mrs. Haynes found that asking students to take photos of the Glenville community was a powerful assignment that included all four stages of the curation process.

Mrs. Haynes writes, "Reading *The Hate U Give* and similar texts helped guide students into articulating their thoughts and trying to understand society through other's words in hopes that they can have better outcomes about issues they face daily. In the book, the main character, Starr, used her voice when her friend was killed by the police officer. She was able to protest and stand up for rights of others. In addition, Starr was able to help other students understand that it is okay to speak your thoughts. She realized that speaking up gave her a stronger stand in her community and at home. She was able to prove that no matter how old you are, you have a voice, so you should use it in a positive way. When students read about Starr and similar characters, they were able to analyze how they can also use their voice and speak up when facing an issue in their community, school, and at home.

"We noticed that many of the students creatively activated their voices through songs, poetry, writing letters, and watching more documentary series to gain knowledge of the history and why we continuously have the same issues in this country. They seemed more able to use their voices positively in grade level meetings at school and in class discussions.

"We developed an assignment that asked students to use mobile devices, including cell phones, cameras, and tablets, to go in the community to take snapshots of what they see. This task was given to them because when we talk about history and issues, we have to look at our surroundings to understand why we face certain issues. We have to look back at our history and how history changed over time. When history changes over time, so do the communities we live in, as do family dynamics, the economy and much more. I wanted the students to understand their community, not just the school they attend daily but the people in the community and how the community is set up.

"Normally, students walk to school and back home, not paying attention to what they see every day. I wanted the students to capture their community and use their voices to help describe pros and cons in their community. One of the students who walked her community took pictures of abandoned buildings and homes. This made her very angry because she really never paid attention to how many abandoned buildings were along the way to school. In conversations, she would mention that she felt sad about what she saw—why did her community have to look so abandoned and why did the community not get rid of the buildings that are making the community look so unpleasant? The student was able to create a video based on the photos she took and how she felt about what she saw in her community. The video was later used in our presentation at a national conference. This gave her and the other students confidence about using their voices to speak up about the issues occurring in her community." The photos were collected and repurposed into a text that was shared outside of the school, including being described in this book. In addition to still photos, at Glenville, I also saw the creation of motion pictures.

DOCUMENTARY FILM

Film (in this case I'm using the term "film" when I might be talking about a video) seems to be a natural form for repurposing. The medium of film brings together so many different forms of representation and even the element of dreams (Metz, 1974/1991). Using films in the English classroom has received validation from NCTE from the very beginning of motion pictures (Kist, 2008). There are many books that have sought to help teachers to help students "read" films (Baker, 2017; Costanzo, 2004; Golden, 2001, 2006; Krueger & Christel, 2001; Monaco, 2000; Spottiswoode, 1950/2011). Film and video have long been suggested as entry points to help kids relate to the literary canon. Teachers have used *The Simpsons* to improve student response (Eikmeier, 2008;) they have used film adaptations to hook kids on Shakespeare (Williamson, 2009) and turned *Great Expectations* into a reality TV show (Bucolo, 2011). And film production has been shown to be able to be used simply as a way to improve reading comprehension or writing facility (Bedard & Fuhrken, 2010; Hall & Stahl, 2012; Schmertz, 2016; Young & Rasinski, 2013)

This chapter is more concerned about the way teachers have used film and other media to help students repurpose their experiences with texts. I wrote about a student-produced film festival in Los Angeles back in 2005

(Kist, 2005), and there are so many examples of similar projects, including students who produced films in cooperation with the Austin Film Festival (Bedard & Fuhrken, 2010); or made digital book trailers (Ehret et al., 2016); or made short documentaries about local issues in the community (Ranker & Mills, 2014); or made documentary film adaptations of research papers (Robinson, 2018); or adapted mentor texts into readers theater scripts and then into videos (Young & Rasinski, 2013). As Ehret et al. (2016) pointed out, "Now youth hold their screens up to the world, making meaning alongside and through them, not only on or behind them" (p. 347). Robin Jocius (2016) describes a summer workshop in which they "'read' a series of visual, musical, digital, and multimedia texts, just as we read poems and stories, about the creators' experiences of living in a particular time and place. Then, students took cameras into their homes and communities to record photographs and video footage that told their own stories of living, playing, and growing up within their neighborhoods. . . . As students created their neighborhood stories—occasionally with words, but more often with photographs, video, sound, music, color, special effects, visual effects, writing, and live acting—they developed critical understandings of how symbols and modes come together to make meaning" (Jocius, 2016, p. 16).

Since the onset of more accessible video equipment, students have been assigned to make animations of poems, use storyboards to map out scenes, and to create explanatory videos. Flipgrid (flipgrid.com) makes it easy for students to post quick video syntheses of their readings.

I have recently been assigning my students to make their own YouTube channels. Quoting from my assignment sheet: "Please curate at least three playlists, each with 10–20 YouTube videos that are related to some specific theme that you have been working on. These playlists should consist of videos that have been made by someone else. . . . (Then) create a playlist that includes 3–5 videos (that are each at least 3 minutes long) that you have made yourself. This playlist should be aligned, also, with the topic you are working on. Try to be creative—don't just talk into the camera." I have found this assignment to be as addicting as many of the other assignments in this book are, with some students setting up elaborate YouTube channels including very creative videos that they have made themselves.

What I heard about at Glenville, almost from the beginning, was a film project that far surpassed most YouTube videos. In 2018, native Clevelander and award-winning filmmaker Paul Sapin came to Glenville to make a film on the 1968 Glenville shoot-out.

Paul Sapin grew up in Cleveland. His father worked in advertising and designed an ad that was used to promote justice for Fred Ahmed Evans, one of the "New Libyans" who was put on trial for murder. Sapin found a poster of one of his father's ads being sold at a gallery in New York, and it renewed his interest in the Glenville shoot-out. He provided the details in a recent interview: "I went to Cleveland. What are the pieces left of this event? Who's around? Who might speak to me? Very quickly, I began to realize rather than having the usual thing, I wondered if it was possible to try this from a different angle—very few people know about the Glenville shoot-out. It's another example of African American history that has been buried" (personal communication, Paul Sapin, September 20, 2021).

Sapin was introduced to Jacqueline Bell, principal of Glenville, who introduced him to Shanita Horton, one of the English teachers with whom I worked. Sapin said, "I thought, let's not have just an older generation tell this story. Let's have this current generation actually research, dig up and try to tell the story." And so they did. The students in Ms. Horton's 12th-grade English class went to work. Since many of the people involved with the Glenville shoot-out were very young in 1968, some were still alive and willing to be interviewed. While being filmed by Sapin, the students conducted interviews in the Glenville neighborhood with many witnesses. They also took a field trip to the Western Reserve Historical Society. "All of the educators I encountered inspired the film making process by promoting the idea that the students themselves could investigate the events of 1968 by embarking on their own research project," Sapin recalls. "I was told by their teachers that these students were bright, but hadn't necessarily shown much interest in school. And now they were; they wanted to know. . . . These were young people who were learning about a very important part of their history, that had happened in their neighborhood, that nobody had told them about."

As of this writing, the film is in post-production, and it is a source of pride for those who took part. As Sapin describes the experience, "There's always more than one narrative. There's always more than one story. It depends on who's telling it and why they're telling it. That was part of their [the students'] educational experience. They could see that there had been an impact to what took place 50 years earlier, and it had largely been

---

GUIDING QUESTIONS FOR REPURPOSING

Is the repurposing compatible with the original texts that are being repurposed?

Is the repurposing original (not heavily influenced by teachers or peers)?

Is the repurposing adding to the conversation (not detracting)?

What is the depth of the reader's repurposing as they envision it?

Has the student made visceral connections between the text and their personal lived experiences, and are they stating the repercussions of the original texts on their life?

(Adapted from Purves et al., 1990, as quoted in White & Lemieux, 2017)

punishing for the community. These conversations have to happen, and when they don't, the people who are shortchanged are the young. They're the ones we're responsible for and to, in that community. They've been denied on a number of fronts."

Whether the repurposing is a poster, a snapshot, or a professional quality documentary film, the point is that students get a chance to reformulate something they've been studying rather than to regurgitate it. So much for what passes as "assessment" in our schools involves a form of memorization (or worse, in that there is no performative purpose!) In my own classrooms and the classrooms I witnessed at Glenville, there has been a spirit of repurposing, an impetus to remix, an urge to make something new. And, ultimately, a need to reflect, which is the focus of the final stage of the curation process.

CHAPTER 5

Reflecting

This fourth step serves as a pause to think about what has been learned, what growth has occurred as a result of the first three steps, and what might be the next goals for curating. What gaps in the learning are there? Where does the learner need to go next? What, finally, has the learner learned? Students may find that reflection is the most important step in the process, as this is the step in which they begin to self-actualize and set their own goals for learning and growth.

The Reflecting stage of the curation process is perhaps the most challenging to operationalize. The key is in the first sentence of the above description—to "pause." In our fast-paced educational climate, it's difficult to find time to "pause" to do anything. But if students are not pausing to take stock of what has been accomplished and what needs to be accomplished, then what is the point of curating to begin with? So we must make time for our students to stop and reflect, and persuade them that it is necessary to find quiet moments.

An additional challenge to operationalizing reflection is that the predominant paradigm for our classrooms frames students as waiting for validation from the teacher in the form of a grade. If there is no grade, then the activity doesn't matter. Any teacher has heard the question, "Is this for a grade?" or "Does this count for anything?" One advantage of the curation model as I'm conceptualizing it is that the validation for what has been learned rests with the student, not the teacher. The problem is that our traditional schools just aren't set up for this. From a very young age, kids are looking for the approval in the form of a grade from a teacher. Breaking out of that routine is difficult.

One way that many teachers get around this is by slapping a grade on the reflection. I think what happens then is that we get a lot of phony reflecting: "Dear Mr. Smith, I have really grown from doing this research paper, I now know how to cite using APA, and this has been life changing!" The teacher gives the student an A for "reflection" and moves on to the next student. How can we inspire more authentic student reflection?

There are two influences, as I see it, that we should be paying more attention to—visual art educators and writing center educators. I think these two groups of educators have been successful in fostering authentic reflection in their students. One of the keys to their success is the one-on-one conference, something that I saw often at Glenville. Teachers at Glenville would pull aside a student for what appeared to be very serious conversations, sometimes about schoolwork, sometimes about life, sometimes about a mixture of the two. This ability to conference was aided by the 80-minute block schedule. The class sizes were relatively small, and the long class periods afforded time for this. Students had enough time to complete assignments and engage with teachers. This time to conference seemed to pay off as evidenced by the deep teacher–student relationships I witnessed. I was always impressed by how well the Glenville teachers knew their students and their challenges. The teachers seemed to really know the students and what they might be going through at home. I think the longer class periods and small class sizes allowed teachers to have time simply to ask students how they were doing and ask about missing assignments.

Ironically, there is much in the literature about how we need teachers to be reflective about their own practice! The two pioneering scholars of teacher reflection were Van Manen (1977) and Schön (1983). They each developed protocols of reflection that take time for teachers to work through. The "lesson study" concept, from Japan, also mandates time be set aside for looking back at one single lesson and reflecting on what happened and what might be changed in the future (Lewis et al., 2012). Except in art classrooms and in what are referred to as "writing centers," however, I rarely remember seeing any such time being advocated for student reflection.

ARTS AND REFLECTION

I think what sets art educators apart from traditional educators is that there is time set aside to reflect. It's not a quick add-on at the end of a unit or lesson. The bottom line is that there must be time for students to think about what they've curated. And not just in some thrown-together exit slip. Embedded in that time set aside for reflection is the implicitly and explicitly stated principle that the teacher cares about what the student thinks. Eisner (1979) famously wrote that "the problem of communicating to some public—parents, school board members, students, state agencies—about what has happened in schools, the problem of making known what is strong and what is weak, what needs support and what does not, can be usefully conceived as an artistic problem" (p. 186). Sadly, some 40 years after Eisner wrote these words, little has changed.

> ### TRADING PLACES
>
> Each student writes their name on one side of an index card. On the back, they write one or more things learned during the lesson and/or any questions. Students then circulate the room and exchange cards with a number of partners. Each student first reads the back of their card and then gives it to their partner. The partner does the same. Each student then has in their possession the card from the last person talked to and goes and talks to another partner, reading the back of the card in their possession. That card is then exchanged with the current partner, and they both move on to new partners. After exchanging cards with a certain number of people (determined by the teacher), each student returns to their seat and tries to write down as many ideas and/or questions as they can remember from all the cards they saw.
>
> (Adapted from Silberman, 1996)

Most art teachers in K–12 settings are able to live in both worlds—the world of aesthetic self-evaluation and the world of assigning grades. The first step in the process of engendering reflection is, of course, to ask the student: How do you feel about this experience? Was it positive or negative? Was it a growth experience or a regression? Because students are often hesitant to really open up about their reflections, I've used reflection protocols such as Trading Places. This is a simple debriefing activity that is low stress. I often use this activity at the end of a unit or a grading period.

Once a quick protocol such as Trading Places is accomplished, I ask students to write in response to some of the following questions:

How have you grown during the past few weeks?
What are you most proud of—Collecting? Organizing? Repurposing?
    All of the above? Explain.
What do you need to work on?

Sometimes I ask students to answer these questions in the form of a reflective letter, but I try not to place too many expectations on this part of the Curation process, because I've noticed that students try to flatter me or "kiss up" by saying how wonderful the last few weeks have been. I don't want that. I want honest reflection, and sometimes that's hard to achieve when the person reading the reflection is the person assigning the grades. For me, the smoothing over of this power differential often can come about during a one-on-one conference.

CONFERENCING

Of course, a major challenge for teachers who do not teach in a block scheduling format is how to arrange for one-on-one conferences when the number of students being worked with is huge. If you see 120 students per day broken into 45-minute periods, it's close to impossible to have any kind of one-on-one conferencing in person. I do believe that technology has given us some answers that we didn't have in earlier decades. Some of the one-on-one conferencing can be achieved through email dialogue. There might even be some students who might prefer to dialogue with the teacher online rather than in person. I realize that most teachers couldn't handle having email dialogues with 120 students at one time, either. Many writing teachers solve this problem by staggering when assignments are due. Teachers can set up schedules in which they are conferencing online with only 10–20 students during any given week.

Whether the conference is held in person or digitally, the foundation for the conversation is the reflective letter referred to in the Organizing chapter and/or the questions listed above. In a curation-based classroom, it is an expectation from the beginning of the school year that the burden of assessment is going to be equally shared by the teachers and the student. Before the conference, the student must take the time to reflect on the curation work that has transpired.

When answering self-reflection questions, students should be encouraged to revisit their learning logs and the various drafts of their work. The self-reflection should be based on the experience of the work, not only the product. Hurst (2005) found that oral sharing of learning logs was effective. Ask students to read out loud portions of their learning logs that point to growth or to the need for more growth.

I believe an important consideration when conferencing with a student is the concept of "flow." Mihaly Csikszentmihalyi (1997, 1993, 1990) studied the optimal experiences of a cross-section of artists, athletes, and craftsmen, and found similarities in their descriptions of their peak experiences—similarities that cut across activities: "A matching of challenges and skills, clear goals, and immediate feedback, resulting in a deep concentration that prevents worry and the intrusion of unwanted thoughts into consciousness, and in a transcendence of the self, are the universal characteristics associated with enjoyable activities" (Csikszentmihalyi, 1990, p. 131). He named this state "flow."

When one is deeply immersed in collecting, organizing, and repurposing something that one cares about, I believe that one experiences this kind of flow state, or at the very least the kind of reading engagement that Guthrie and Wigfield (1997) described. Reading was actually found to be a (leading) cause of flow (Massimini et al., 1988). I saw some "flow" happening in the Glenville classrooms, and I feel that I've seen students achieve a flow state occasionally in my own classroom. I suppose the ultimate question that a teacher could ask a student is: Did you feel that you achieved a flow state at any time during these 9 weeks? If so, when? If not, why not? What do you need to do so that you are more deeply engrossed with your work more often? "It is by being fully involved with every detail of our lives, whether good or bad, that we find happiness" (Csikszentmihalyi, 1990, p. 2).

Once students are familiar with flow, I can ask: During any of the stages of curation were you in a "flow" state? Did you lose track of time? Did you forget to stop working? Were you angry when you needed to stop working? If the answer to any of those questions is yes, then that is a good sign. A follow-up question to ask then is where the student wants to go next. What will put you in that "flow" state again? If I don't feel that students are ready to understand and self-reflect regarding flow, I might ask questions such as: Did you lose track of time and forget to stop working? Were you so focused that you didn't notice what was going on around you? Were you even angry when someone told you to stop? If they say Yes, they probably achieved flow. And they will want to get back to it, so I ask: What do you think you can do to get to this flow state again? The bottom line is that I hope that the heightened engagement I've designed curation for leads to the "flow" state for my students.

But beyond trying to find the pleasurable "flow" state, it's important to challenge the student on what needs to be improved in the work. Certainly, arts educators do this constantly, and so do composition teachers. In Atwell's (2015) model, the writer/artist is supposed to be ready before the conference with a list of things that the teacher/responder should be looking for. Again, the burden is on the student, not the teacher, to identify things to work on. Atwell has a long list of possible issues to bring up with a responder, from looking at the introduction, the body, and the conclusion, to looking at logic and structure and even mechanics issues.

The danger with modeling our Reflection stage too much on the Writing Center approach is that we want to be careful not to go overboard on constructing rubrics or protocols that defeat the purpose of the student-centered curation process. While we might be proud of the rubric we have designed, we have to make sure our rubric is not, in the end, just another way of restricting student experience, boiling everything down to what the kids need to do to get an A (Kohn, 2006). As Kohn has written, "Rubrics are, above all, a tool to promote standardization, to turn teachers into grading machines or at least allow them to pretend that what they are doing is exact and objective" (Kohn, 2006, p. 12). The bottom line is that we know that, during this most crucial phase of the curation process, we teachers need to be present, but we also need to tread lightly.

One thing we can learn from the Atwell approach is that there should be input, during the Reflection stage, not only from the teacher. As Player (2021) has written (crediting Anzaldúa [1983] for the idea), "It is critical that teachers allow students to share their writing with one another, not only for surface purposes like peer editing, but to provide opportunities for students to teach and learn with and from one another as they build the intimacy that arises from sharing stories" (p. 237). Player describes an afterschool program for girls of color called The Unnormal Sisterhood, suggesting that literacy experiences both in and out of school should be "reshaped to simultaneously center girls of color and other minoritized identities and knowledges, while also providing space for those knowledges to be used toward critical work. One step forward would be to invite a variety of genres, thereby providing opportunities for girls to write from personal experience, with emotion, and without the constraints of the over-structured five-paragraph essays that are so predominant in schools, and particularly schools that serve youth of color" (p. 237). I believe that I saw the essence of these recommendations carried out during the school day in ELA classrooms at Glenville. The process of reading, writing, and responding to a variety of texts seemed to be a breath of fresh air for the students and teachers I've encountered there. Because the students could read, write, and respond to a wide variety of texts without strict limits, they felt freer and they enjoyed their work more than students with tighter constraints.

Leekeenan and White (2021) recently described the writing groups that they set up in their diverse high schools. "Our students . . . faced anti-Black, anti-Latinx policies and linguistic prejudice, resulting in trauma. As writing teachers, we believe writing can be a means for self-discovery, activism, and healing from these traumas" (Leekennan & White, 2021, p. 92). Recognizing this, they researched writing groups with their students and then organized their own groups. These were small student-led groups often centered on a theme or set of themes. "The more we learned about communities of writers, the stronger our belief became that writing groups could destabilize a teacher's role as the arbiter of knowledge and strengthen students' ownership of their stories" (Leekeenan & White, 2021, p. 93). Whether a writing group is set up or whether just one "critical friend" is established, it probably is important to allow students to read each other's work during the reflection stage, so that the long-ingrained pattern of only caring about what the teacher thinks is broken.

There are times when students just are not adept at Reflecting or are even resistant to it. In these cases, the teacher may need to resort to more of an old-school rubric or checklist so that a grade can be assigned. I have adapted a checklist that can be used in these situations from the work of Beach et al. (2016).

CHECKLIST OF QUESTIONS TO ASK DURING THE REFLECTION STAGE

Has the student contextualized the texts that have been **collected** both in terms of their origins and within the student's own inquiry trajectory?

Has the student obviously spent time with a number of texts as reflected in their learning log?

In the **organization** of texts, has the student taken on a defined perspective or stance? Are there clear purposes or themes evident in organizations?

Is there an adequate level of intertextuality (looking at themes and ideas across forms of representation)?

In the **repurposing**, is there a clear link to the Multimodal Memoir? Are there clear autobiographical connections?

Has there been a clear effort to **reflect**? Are there "highs" and "lows" described? Is it clear where the student wants to go next?

Adapted from Beach et al., 2016

GUIDING QUESTIONS FOR THE REFLECTION STAGE

How have you grown during the past few weeks?

What are you most proud of—Collecting? Organizing? Repurposing? All of the above? Explain.

What do you need to work on?

Did you experience being in a "flow" state? If so, when?

What did you learn?

What surprised you?

What have you learned about yourself?

If you were king of the world, what would you do next?

Setting your sights more realistically (than being king of the world), what would you do next?

The reflection stage is, by necessity, the most idiosyncratic stage. Students need to be given time and space to reflect in the ways they prefer. It's not surprising when students have difficulty truly reflecting on their work. They've never been asked to do so before except in the most cursory ways. Students are rarely asked their opinions about their own work and where they want to go next with their work. And on top of this challenge, we humans are sometimes not that honest with ourselves. The reflection stage takes time to implement properly. And time is, unfortunately, in short supply.

CHAPTER 6

Summing Up

When I'm writing, I sometimes listen to music, always something without lyrics. For some random reason, I've been listening to Brahms while writing this book, mainly the Piano Concerto No. 1 in D minor. It's the performance by Rudolf Serkin with the Cleveland Orchestra, from 1968. I have several hundred vinyl recordings in my home office that I like to listen to when I'm working, because it's the only place I have a turntable.

I just grabbed this album when I started writing this book, because I was in the mood to write to classical music. For some reason, the music ended up matching the topic for me, especially the first entrance of the piano in the first movement as the piano suddenly is completely alone, sounding a poignant, nostalgic theme. The music affected me so much that I looked again at the record cover to read more about this concerto. I discovered inside the cover that I had saved a program from a performance of this concerto in 1983. That must be why I have this album. I'd seen this concerto performed at Blossom Music Center, the summer outdoor home of the Cleveland Orchestra. I'm glad that I saved that program because it makes the music more meaningful to me. I have no memory of whom I was with that evening—August 26, 1983. The guest conductor was Sir Andrew Davis. And the soloist was John Lill.

To help me procrastinate, I did some research into Brahms. Interestingly, he was someone who was accused of "remixing." Brahms's First Symphony was compared with Beethoven's Ninth, complete with a similar hymnlike "Ode to Joy" theme at the end. When someone pointed out the similarities, Brahms replied "Any ass can hear that" (Ross, 2010). I have felt sympatico with Brahms as I have been writing this book, because I feel that this book is a remix, a remix of my own work with the work of the Glenville teachers and the work of the community.

The work that I've been doing with the Glenville teachers has taken me back in time, to my own earliest days of teaching, when I saw my own students completely engrossed watching Charlie Chaplin's *The Kid*. It's hard to believe that those kids are now middle-aged. What did they take away from that experience, if anything? I'm guessing that I've been more moved by the experience than they were. It's the same with the Glenville teachers.

I think they wonder about the impact they are having, especially when they hear about a former or current student experiencing some kind of tragedy. Riffing with the Glenville teachers gave me a chance to unpack some materials from years ago and to put them into new curation containers: collecting, organizing, repurposing, and reflecting.

Also, my retirement from Kent State University prompted me over the past few years to attempt to digitize as many of my files as possible. Writing this book would have been much more challenging if I had not gone through that process, if I had not realized that my past organizational system was not giving me the access I needed. This also coincided with the onset of the pandemic, which meant I was doing more online coaching and teaching; if I had not digitized many of my files and articles, I would have not been able to serve the teachers and students with whom I've been working as efficiently, or at all. It made me wonder what I would have done if I had to do this remixing if I was still plowing through paper copies. The attention I gave to curation of my various texts over the last few years has been a good thing.

During this same period, with my own children, I'd had the eerie experience of seeing them play with some object I'd purchased for a completely different purpose years before they were born or, in the case of our old family piano, years before even I was born. I felt that these steps of curation were processes that they did naturally and that we did together as a family. As those of us who were fortunate stayed home during the onset of the pandemic and students were forced to be at least somewhat self-sufficient, I felt that thinking and writing about the process of curation made sense. Perhaps brick-and-mortar schools will look different in a post-pandemic world. Perhaps students will be expected to take charge of their own learning, curating their own literacy lives, instead of having their lives curated for them by the teacher, by the curriculum, by standardized tests, by politicians.

Writing this book has been a kind of meditation for me, all set off by Ms. Davis's directing her students to go to their phones. It's given me a chance to explore what I have curated over the years. And to riff with some fellow riffers! I felt joy and camaraderie in the combinations that we came up with. As I would bring materials to the Glenville teachers, they would bring ideas to me. It became a conversation that continues to this day and has been preserved in this book.

This chapter summarizes some of the key themes from the curation model, the work of the Glenville teachers, and the past pandemic years of online teaching. I'm guessing most classroom teachers who read this won't be in a position to transform their classrooms into multimodal curation workshops. For those who are, go for it, and please let me know how it goes! For those who can't, I do believe there are some "baby steps" (that aren't really trivial) that can be taken.

COLLECTING

Probably every parent knows what their child enjoys collecting. When our daughter Mariel was very young, she enjoyed collecting rocks. She would pick up interesting rocks wherever she went. We soon realized that we needed a container for all of her rocks. We provided her with an old pot that used to contain a plant. Soon the container was filled with rocks.

About this same time, Mariel's sister, Vivienne, was stating a very strong preference for the color pink. I believe in an effort to set herself apart from her sister, Mariel started being very clear that her favorite color is green. Soon after, Mariel started saying that she loved avocados. Once people knew of this interest, people started giving her clothing and various items that were decorated with avocados. As Mariel's collecting interests grew, we tried to grow with her, providing her with the support she needed, from something as trivial to giving her a container for her rocks to making sure we always had a few avocados in the house.

When Vivienne started taking art lessons, we decided to put her artwork up on a wall of our home. It became Viv's "art wall," and soon we added another wall for Liam's work, and then one for Mariel. Also, at the suggestion of Viv's art teacher, Jennifer Davis, started keeping an art journal—a collection of some of her favorite pieces of art as well as some of her own drawings. We purchased a binder and some sheet protectors for Viv's art journal and soon found that it was a great thing to do for each of our kids. They had an easy receptacle for the pieces of art that meant something to them, whether created by them or by someone else.

In addition, both Stephanie and I have shared our own collections with our children, sharing the joy we feel with collecting certain items. Stephanie has a number of heirloom quilts and other homemade items. I have an office filled with books, graphic novels, and music to share.

I think what I have learned from being a parent and working with the Glenville teachers is that there needs to be some flexibility in the texts we allow our students and children to collect. What we see as clutter in our homes and in our classrooms might actually be "the very fiber of their beings." I'm not talking about hoarding here. I'm saying that there must be some room in our classrooms and our homes for inquiry. One-size-fits-all curriculum is a turnoff, and few seem to acknowledge that. This is odd since so many of us remember the horror of marching lockstep through some canonical text. Why do we want to keep doing this to our kids? Let them collect!

And today's teachers have so many more convenient ways of administering collecting than I did, much of it clutter free! I certainly wish I could have had my students each set up a Goodreads account (www.goodreads.com). What a simple, quick way for teachers to monitor choice reading! No more paper-based reading logs! Assigning a grade to choice reading doesn't have to be a chore—you, as the teacher, can have a Goodreads account as well and model that you have your own reading life, forming a community of readers with your students. Goodreads also can be an answer for the teacher who lacks time for choice reading. Just do it all online; perhaps make it an option for students who want to earn alternative credit. If teachers can allow for even 15 minutes of choice reading per week, this will probably make more of an impact than anything else that is going on in class that week (Kohn, 2010; Krashen, 2013). Even just starting the class with a 5-minute discussion on "What are you currently reading for fun?" can be deliciously subversive (in a totally good way).

ORGANIZING

I think one of the most challenging aspects of the Organizing stage of curation is that often our kids' conceptions of "organizing" are different from our conception. And yet, if we impose some organizational structure on them, how will they learn to organize as independent creators? Don't be afraid to let the kids get messy with their organizing. Again, the technology allows sufficient "space" for kids to organize however they see fit. Be open to changing organizational patterns.

We've noticed that our children tend to change their organizational systems quite often. Our son, Liam, who must have at least 500 Hot Wheels and Matchbox cars, sometimes organizes his vehicles by color, sometimes by make or model, or sometimes by their function in whatever diorama he's working on. It's the same with his LEGOs. Instead of keeping his LEGOs together in whatever set they were originally part of, he chooses to put all of his LEGO together in one bin and then organize them by function depending on whatever he is building. We sometimes ask, when he receives a new LEGO kit (let's say for a Batmobile), "Are you sure you don't want to leave all of these pieces together in a separate bag?" He will always say no, and we honor that.

The bottom line is that there has to be space for kids to organize in their own way (while recognizing norms of keeping things clean and safe for others). There has to be room for them to organize in their own way, so that if it's anathema to the way in which you want your home to be organized, try to make sure there is a dedicated space for your children's curating activities. We realize that we are lucky to have a dedicated playroom for our kids to have space for their various organizational systems.

REPURPOSING

We are all familiar with kids who are more excited about the boxes than they are about the toy. Liam uses boxes for buildings or sometimes something we would never expect. He uses old Pringles cans for silos. He repurposes other people's trash and other items to make a landscaping crew truck that is straight out of the Little Rascals. He repurposes other people's logos and business cards.

Our daughters paint their Barbies. They use paint and markers on things like putty and various toys. Mariel likes to put the tip of a marker on a paper towel or napkin; the ink spreads out making designs. She takes computer paper and staples to repurpose into houses and buildings.

They use old dress-up clothes rather than a store-bought costume as a princess. They mix and match stuff all the time. In fact, I am hard pressed to think of a traditional toy that our kids play with exactly as it was intended, except for things like Magna-Tiles or Tinkertoys, and even with these toys, several Magna-Tiles might find their way into a creation largely composed of LEGOs, supplemented with a few Lincoln Logs thrown in. In short, we try to allow for repurposing as much as possible as long as it doesn't totally destroy the toy, the house, or the children!

Again, it is sometimes difficult for teachers to find room for Repurposing. But there are models out there. Based, supposedly, upon the idea that big tech companies, such as Google, allow their employees up to 20% of their time to work on their own projects, "Genius Hour" is a movement that allows kids (and teachers) some time and space within the school day to follow their passions. Schools are increasingly building regularly scheduled Genius Hour time into their schedules for what equate to inquiry projects (Simos, 2015). So many schools are trying out some form of a block schedule, and I regularly hear teachers complain that they don't know how to fill 80-minute block periods. Why not consider setting up a Genius Hour once a week to fill up one of your big block periods? Allowing students some time to follow their own interests might not actually be that subversive in this era of "capstone projects" because work they do during Genius Hour could serve to stimulate future capstone projects (which Ohio now counts as an alternative path to graduation). And letting kids follow their passions is certainly not a new educational idea, as writers for centuries have described the benefits of this kind of unscripted, interdisciplinary inquiry (Dewey, 1934/1980; Holt, 1967/1995; Rousseau, 1762/1979).

Back in 2012, I published a model for a multimodal workshop that could be set up even during a traditional brick-and-mortar school day (Kist, 2012). With more schools going to online instruction, there might not be the need to attach minutes to each of these components. But at least this

Model for a New Literacies Workshop

Time for Mini-Lessons

Direct Instruction
Lecture/Discussion
Guided Instruction
Other Models

Covering various "standards statements" in the Core Curriculum that need to be covered, and as needed by students.

This time could also be spent on equipping students with various critical literacy skills/stances (Bean & Moni, 2003; Heffernan & Lewis, 2009; Tan & Guo, 2010).

This time could also be spent on troubleshooting projects and creative works, or on equipping students with knowledge of how to work in various forms of representation (providing tutorials, for example, on how to work with a particular animation software).

Time for Reading and Responding	**Time for Reading and Responding**
To Teacher-Chosen Texts (literary and informational)	**To Student-Chosen Texts** (literary and informational)
Reading Page-based texts Screen-based texts	**Reading** Page-based texts Screen-based texts
Related Topics from Common Core Reading Strand *Reading for key ideas and details Reading for craft and structure Reading for integration of knowledge and ideas Range of reading and level of text complexity*	***Related Topics from Common Core Reading Strand*** *Reading for key ideas and details Reading for craft and structure Reading for integration of knowledge and ideas Range of reading and level of text complexity*
Responding Using page-based texts Using screen-based, multimodal texts such as: blogging, posting on a discussion board, creating a new text (video, podcast, VoiceThread, etc.)	**Responding** Using page-based texts Using screen-based, multimodal texts such as: blogging, posting on a discussion board, creating a new text (video, podcast, VoiceThread, etc.)

Related Topics from **Common Core Writing & Language Strands**	Related Topics from **Common Core Writing & Language Strands**
Text types and purposes *Production and distribution of writing* *Research to Build and Present knowledge* *Range of Writing* *Conventions of Standard English* *Knowledge of Language* *Vocabulary Acquisition and Use*	*Text types and purposes* *Production and distribution of writing* *Research to Build and Present knowledge* *Range of Writing* *Conventions of Standard English* *Knowledge of Language* *Vocabulary Acquisition and Use*

Time for Writing/Creating	**Time for Writing/Creating**
Teacher-Directed Texts Creating page-based texts Creating screen-based texts	**Student-Directed Texts** Creating page-based texts Creating screen-based texts
Related Topics from **Common Core Writing & Language Strands** *Text types and purposes* *Production and distribution of writing* *Research to Build and Present knowledge* *Range of Writing* *Conventions of Standard English* *Knowledge of Language* *Vocabulary Acquisition and Use*	Related Topics from **Common Core Writing & Language Strands** *Text types and purposes* *Production and distribution of writing* *Research to Build and Present knowledge* *Range of Writing* *Conventions of Standard English* *Knowledge of Language* *Vocabulary Acquisition and Use*

Time to Exhibit and Archive Work

Related Topics from Common Core Speaking and Listening Strand
Comprehension and Collaboration
Presentation of Knowledge and Ideas

Just as writing workshops use the Author's Chair strategy (Graves & Hansen, 1983), most teachers I've researched carve out some time for students to exhibit their work in whatever form they are working in. These exhibitions may take the form of page-based exhibitions or screen-based exhibitions (such as wikis, theatrical presentations, visual art exhibits, etc.).

structure can still provide some guidance and was remarkably resonant with
what the Glenville teachers did within the school day.

REFLECTING

I think many parents have had the experience of realizing, quite suddenly,
"Everything seems very quiet." That can be a signal for worry—perhaps the
kids are so engrossed because they are making a mess or breaking a rule.
But in fact we often find that our children have stumbled onto some kind of
repurposing or invention that is new to them. Sometimes it might manifest
itself as more interest in the box than what the box contained. I've seen
my son repurpose various containers to become platforms for an elevated
Hot Wheels track. Or certainly playing with water or dirt in some newfan-
gled way can become a stimulus for minutes if not hours of engrossed play.
Stephanie and I try to enable as much of that kind of "flow"-producing
activity as possible, and then we debrief about it. What was fun about this?
What would you like to do again? What tools and other items do you need
to improve the experience? We aren't always so level-headed, but we do try
to validate the fact that often the manufactured store-bought toys aren't as
interesting as what the kids' own minds can create and repurpose.

We talk a lot at mealtimes. We do put the devices and toys away during
mealtime and talk about what we are all doing. We make sure the kids understand that this talking that we do is as important and vital as the eating.
Even if they are not hungry, we expect them to come to the table and talk.
Sometimes we use a protocol such as "roses and thorns"—asking kids to
report a "rose" (good thing) and a "thorn" (bad thing) that happened during the day. Sometimes we just free-associate.

Another reflection aid we use is photo albums. We still print out some
hard-copy photographs and put them in photo albums. We find that our
children enjoy going through old photos and talking about past experiences.
We put some of our spare photos in a big box that the kids are free to use for
whatever purpose. Sometimes they will use them to make collages or gifts
for people. This also allows them to debrief and think and talk about past
events. Mariel also keeps several journals in which she writes occasionally,
although this doesn't seem to be part of her daily routine.

Sometimes I think one of the most powerful reflection aids for students
is for a teacher to notice some detail in a student's work. This noticing can
sometimes set the student off on a quick reflection about what that noticing
has meant. I noticed what the Glenville teachers have been doing. I called it
out and named it. I reflected on the work they have been doing, and I think
they have, too. I think there is a human aspect to the curation model that is
needed in our "data-driven" schools.

As I pack up and get ready to leave Glenville, I look across the street where there are some old apartment buildings. It looks like the buildings have been there for years. They are still solid structures with big stone facades and big open balconies outside each apartment. There are apparently five apartments in each building—two on the second floor, two on the first floor and one in the basement. My eye is always caught by the apartment on the left of the first floor. Whoever lives there has quite a decorating talent. Each season of the year, there is a fun remix of flags, figurines, signs, and hanging items such as wind chimes. The aesthetic sense that the occupant demonstrates in the way the balcony is curated is very impressive. I sometimes even stop on the street when I'm driving by to look at all of the interesting ephemera. I notice that none of the neighbors decorate their balconies. Just this one person. I wonder who that person is and what the inspiration was for this ongoing, everchanging display. If I ever see that person outside, I am going to stop and say thank you for giving me a little joy each time I visit Glenville.

Multimodal Memoir

This assignment encourages you to think about all the various texts of your life as they relate to reading and writing. Your own history as a reader, writer, and viewer of various texts will have a significant impact on your future literacy experiences. Doing the following exercise should help you reflect on your own multimodal textual past.

Your objective is to create a screen-based representation of the influence of these various texts on your life from childhood to today. Such texts may include books, films, television shows, music, newspapers, magazines, sports, restaurants, food, cars, fashion, architecture, and interior design (to name a few examples.) Visit Google Images, Flickr, Yahoo Image Search, YouTube, etc., and find some images or video clips related to the important texts of your life. You might want to start with the book you shared during your video introduction and then riff off that.

You may create this assignment in any one of the following programs: VoiceThread (http://voicethread.com); PowerPoint; Prezi; or digital storytelling tools such as Storymaker (https://www.story-maker.org/), Umajin (http://www.umajin.com/), or MixBook (http://www.mixbook.com); or create a comic book portrayal of a character or yourself using Comic Life (http://plasq.com/comiclife).

You will be assessed based on:

1. Have you presented some specific and important texts related to your literacy past from your childhood through adulthood? Does your memoir appear to have been just thrown together at the last minute, or has some real thought gone into it? What evidence is there that you have thought about the themes or storylines that run throughout your textual uses? Are these themes and/or storylines clearly presented or are they still in process? (30 points)
2. Has some creativity gone into the creation of the memoir? (10 points)
   Did you build a presentation with innovative use of graphics and/or music?
   Did some thought go into the graphic design used in the slides or video?

Were there some relevant, interesting music clips included?
Were there some uses of sound effects?
Were there some video clips included?
Was there some imagination displayed (humor, pathos, interest-
ing juxtaposition of images and/or sound, etc.)?
(Please note: not all of these elements must be included.)

3. In your presentation, how thoroughly do you present a reflection
on the place non–print-dominated media have played related
to your language learning? Are there a variety of kinds of texts
represented? Have you reflected on lessons you have learned from
your multimodal past? (30 points)

4. Do you make implications for how reflecting on your multimodal
past might shape your current and future literacy experiences? (20
points)

5. Is your presentation at least 5 minutes long? (10 points)

MULTIMODAL MEMOIR QUESTIONS TO CONSIDER

Below are some prompts to help you get started writing your multimodal
literacy memoir:

1. Can you recall reading for pleasure in elementary school?
2. Can you remember writing for pleasure in elementary school?
3. Can you remember the first time you noticed that either you
were using different words from others to describe something, or
someone else was?
4. Can you recall the first book you chose to read in elementary
school?
5. Can you recall your first writing assignment in elementary school?
6. Did you have a library card when you were in elementary school?
Did you use it then? What did you check out from the library,
predominantly? In later school years?
7. Can you recall the first book you loved (couldn't put down)?
8. Can you recall the first film or television show you loved and
watched over and over again?
9. Can you remember a great speech that you heard presented live?
10. Do you feel that you've ever read a book that has made a
difference in your life?
11. Has a nonprint text made a difference in your life?
12. Have you ever read a book that you knew had been challenged or
censored? How did you feel about reading it?

13. Have you ever encountered a text online that you thought adults would be upset to know that you encountered? How did you feel about encountering that text?
14. Were you a reader in your intermediate and/or junior high or middle school years?
15. How did your reading and writing habits change when you went to school and over the years?
16. Are there any social/cultural/religious organizations associated with writing or reading that you recall?
17. Can you pleasurably recall sharing books with friends?
18. Can you pleasurably recall talking about nonprint texts with friends?
19. Did you read a certain type of book (such as mysteries or biographies) at a particular age? Why do you think you made such choices?
20. Were you required to read certain novels in middle school or high school? How did you feel about that?
21. Is there a specific teacher(s) who stands out in your memory as someone who had an impact on your reading and/or writing?
22. What contributions have your reading and writing abilities made to your life?
23. Are you a reader now?
24. Are you a writer now?
25. What alternative media do you peruse most often now?
26. Do you feel comfortable modeling reading and writing for your students?
27. What are you currently reading? Writing?

Questions adapted from McLaughlin and Vogt (1996) and Brown (1999).

References

Abrams, J. J., Lieber, J., & Lindelof, D. (Creators). (2004–2010). *Lost* [TV series]. ABC Signature; Bad Robot Productions; Touchstone Television.

Achebe, C. (1958/1994). *Things fall apart*. Penguin.

Albers, P. (1997). Art as literacy. *Language Arts, 74*(5), 338–350.

Albers, P. Pace, C. L., & Odo, D. (2016). From affinity and beyond: A study of online literacy conversations and communities. *Journal of Literacy Research, 48*(2), 221–250.

Anderson, K. M., & Mack, R. (2019). Digital storytelling: A narrative method for positive identity development in minority youth. *Social Work With Groups, 42*(1), 43–55.

Anderson, L. H. (1999/2019). *Speak: 20th anniversary edition*. Square Fish.

Anzaldúa, G. (1983). Speaking in tongues: A letter to third world women writers. In C. Moraga & G. Anzaldúa (Eds.), *This bridge called my back: Writings of radical women of color* (2nd ed.) (pp. 165–174). Women of Color Press.

Applebee, A., & Langer, J. (2011). A snapshot of writing instruction in middle schools and high schools. *English Journal, 100*(6), 14–27.

Assaf, L. C., Pakamile, P., & Brooks, J. (2021). Superheroes and community innovators: Opportunities to engage in critical literacy in a makerspace camp in rural South Africa. *Language Arts, 98*(6), 315–329.

Atwell, N. (2015). *In the middle: A lifetime of learning about writing, reading and adolescents (3rd ed.)*. Heinemann.

Autrey, T., Edington, C., Gardner, R., Hicks, T., Kobodian, A., & Russo, A. (2007). Rethinking the purposes and processes for designing digital portfolios. *Journal of Adolescent & Adult Literacy, 50*(6), 450–458.

Bailey, N. M., & Carroll, K. M. (2010). Motivating students' research skills and interests through a multimodal, multigenre research project. *English Journal, 99*(6), 78–85.

Baker, F. W. (2017). *Close reading the media: Literacy lessons and activities for every month of the school year*. Routledge.

Barrish, H. (Producer), & DuVernay, A. (Director). (2016). *The 13th* [Motion picture]. Netflix.

Barton, D., & Hamilton, M. (1998). *Local literacies: Reading and writing in one community*. Routledge.

Batchelor, K. E. (2018a). "My story came to life!": How multimodality can inspire revision in writing. *Gifted Child Today, 41*(3), 136–148.

Batchelor, K. E. (2018b). Using linked text sets to promote advocacy and agency through a critical lens. *Journal of Adolescent & Adult Literacy, 62*(4), 379–386.

Batchelor, K., Kist, W., Kidder-Brown, M., & Bejcek-Long, B. (2015). "Ogres remind me of expanding": First-graders' multimodal autobiographies. *Ubiquity: The Journal of Literature, Literacy, and the Arts, Research Strand*, 2(1), 124–155. http://ed-ubiquity.gsu.edu/wordpress/batchelor-kist-kidder-brown-and-bejcek -long-2-1/

Beach, R., Anson, C., Breuch, L-A., & Reynolds, T. (2014). *Understanding and creating digital texts: An activity-based approach*. Rowman & Littlefield.

Beach, R., Appleman, D., Fecho, B., & Simon, R. (2016). *Teaching literature to adolescents* (3rd ed.). Routledge.

Bean, T. W., & Moni, K. (2003). Developing students' critical literacy: Exploring identity construction in young adult fiction. *Journal of Adolescent & Adult Literacy*, 46, 638–648.

Bedard, C., & Fuhrken, C. (2010). "Everybody wants somebody to hear their story": High school students writing screenplays. *English Journal*, 100(1), 47–52.

Berghoff, B., & Borgmann, C.B. (2007). Imagining new possibilities with our partners in the arts. *English Education*, 40(1), 21–40.

Black, R. W. (2009). Online fan fiction, global identities, and imagination. *Research in the Teaching of English*, 43, 397–425.

Bourne, T. M., & Thomas, A. (Producers), & Tillman, G. (Director). (2018). *The Hate U Give*. [Motion picture]. Fox 2000 Pictures.

Bowen, D. H., Greene, J. P., & Kisida, B. (2014). Learning to think critically: A visual art experiment. *Educational Researcher*, 43(1), 37–44.

Brass, J. (2008). Local knowledge and digital movie composing in an after-school literacy program. *Journal of Adolescent & Adult Literacy*, 51, 464–473.

Bridges, R. (Author), & Lundell, M. (Editor). (1999). *Through my eyes*. Scholastic Press.

Brown, D. (1999). Promoting reflective thinking: Preservice teachers' literacy autobiographies as a common text. *Journal of Adolescent & Adult Literacy*, 42, 402–410.

Bucolo, J. (2011). *Survivor*: *Satis House*: Creating classroom community while teaching Dickens in a reality-TV world. *English Journal*, 100(5), 29–32.

Calkins, L., & Harwayne, S. (1990). *Living between the lines*. Heinemann.

Callahan, M., & King, J. M. (2011). Classroom remix: Patterns of pedagogy in a techno-literacies poetry unit. *Journal of Adolescent & Adult Literacy*, 55, 134–144.

Camangian, P. (2010, November). Starting with self: Teaching autoethnography to foster critically caring literacies. *Research in the Teaching of English*, 45(2), 179–204.

Campano, G., Ghiso, M. P., & Sanchez, L. (2013). "Nobody knows the . . . amount of a person": Elementary students critiquing dehumanization through organic critical literacies. *Research in the Teaching of English*, 48(1), 98–125.

Carroll, L. (2019). *Alice's adventures in wonderland*. Seawolf Press. (Original work published 1865)

Carter, S., Crabapple, M., Batt, J., Boekender, K., & Hampton, D. (2016, September 15). Jay-Z: The war on drugs is an epic fail. *The New York Times*. https://www.nytimes.com/2016/09/15/opinion/jay-z-the-war-on-drugs-is-an -epic-fail.html

Cherry, M. A., Downing Jr., E., & Smith, B. W. (Directors). (2019). *Hair love* [Film]. Matthew A. Cherry Entertainment; Chasing Miles; Lion Forge Animation.

Chisholm, J. S., & Trent, B. (2013). Digital storytelling in a place-based composition course. *Journal of Adolescent & Adult Literacy, 57*, 307–318.

Choudhury, M., & Share, J. (2012). Critical media literacy: A pedagogy for new literacies and urban youth. *Voices From the Middle, 19*(4), 39–44.

Cilesiz, S. (2009). Educational computer use in leisure contexts: A phenomenological study of adolescents' experiences at internet cafes. *American Educational Research Journal, 46*, 232–274.

Cleveland Museum of Art. (n.d.). *ArtLens* [App]. https://www.clevelandart.org /artlens-gallery/artlens-app

Cline, E. (2011). *Ready player one.* Ballantine.

Cohen, J. N., & Mihalidis, P. (2013). Exploring Curation as a core competency in digital and media literacy education. *Faculty Works: Digital Humanities & New Media, 4.* http://digitalcommons.molloy.edu/dhnm_fac/4

Coogler, R. (Director). (2018). *Black panther* [Film]. Marvel Studios, Walt Disney Pictures.

Coombs, D., & Bellingham, D. (2015). Using text sets to foster critical inquiry. *English Journal, 105*(2), 88–95.

Costa, A. L., & Kallick, B. (2008). *Habits of mind.* ASCD.

Costanzo, W. (2004). *Great films and how to teach them.* National Council of Teachers of English.

Costanzo, W. (2008). *The writer's eye: Composition in the multimedia age.* McGraw-Hill.

Crovitz, D., & Moran, C. (2020). Analyzing disruptive memes in an age of international interference. *English Journal, 109*(4), 62–69.

Crovitz, D. (2007). Scrutinizing the cybersell: Teen-targeted web sites as texts. *English Journal, 97*(1), 49–55.

Csikszentmihalyi, M. (1990). *Flow: The psychology of optimal experience.* HarperCollins.

Csikszentmihalyi, M. (1993). *The evolving self: A psychology for the third millennium.* HarperCollins.

Csikszentmihalyi, M. (1997). *Finding flow: The psychology of engagement with everyday life.* Basic Books.

Cuff, S., & Statz, H. (2010). The story of stuff: Reading advertisements through critical eyes. *English Journal, 99*(3), 27–32.

DeJaynes, T. (2015). "Where I'm from" and belonging: A multimodal, cosmopolitan perspective on arts and inquiry. *E-Learning and Digital Media, 12*(2), 183–198.

Delpit, L. (1995). *Other people's children: Cultural conflict in the classroom.* The New Press.

Delpit, L., & Dowdy, J. (Eds.). (2008). *The skin that we speak: Thoughts on language and culture in the classroom.* The New Press.

Dewey, J. (1902/1990). *The school and society.* University of Chicago Press.

Dewey, J. (1934/1980). *Art as experience.* Perigee Books.

Dezuanni, M., O'Mara, J., & Griffith, C. B. (2015). "Redstone is like electricity": Children's performative representations in and around Minecraft. *E-Learning and Digital Media, 12*(2), 147–163.

Doering, A., Beach, R., & O'Brien, D. (2007). Infusing multimodal tools and digital literacies into an English education program. *English Education, 40*, 41–60.

Doerr-Stevens, C. (2015). "That's not something I was, I am, or am ever going to be:" Multimodal self-assertion in digital video production. *E-Learning and Digital Media 12*(2), 164–182.

Dolby Laboratories. (2014). *Silent, a short film*. A Moonbot Studios Production. https://www.youtube.com/watch?v=KA6azZALMiE

Dover, A. G., & Pozdol, T. (2016). Teaching good kids in a m.A.A.d. world: Using hip-hop to reflect, reframe, and respond to complex realities. *English Journal, 105*(4), 43–48.

DuVernay, A. (Director). (2019). *When they see us*. [Motion picture]. Netflix.

Dyson, A. H. (2003). *The brothers and sisters learn to write*. Teachers College Press.

Ehret, C., Hollett, T., & Jocius, R. (2016). The matter of new media making: An intra-action analysis of adolescents making a digital book trailer. *Journal of Literacy Research, 48*(3), 346–377.

Eikmeier, G. M. (2008). D'oh! Using *The Simpsons* to improve student response to literature. *English Journal, 97*(4), 77–80.

Eisenbach, B. B., Corrieri, C., Moniz, K., & Forrester, R. (2018). In search of identity: Connecting the classics to contemporary texts. *Voices From the Middle, 26*(2), 34–38.

Eisner, E. W. (2002). What can education learn from the arts about the practice of education? *The encyclopedia of pedagogy and informal education*. https://infed.org/mobi/what-can-education-learn-from-the-arts-about-the-practice-of-education/

Eisner, E. W. (2005). Opening a shuttered window: An introduction to a special section on the arts and the intellect. *Phi Delta Kappan, 87*(1), 8–10.

Eisner, E. W. (1979). *The educational imagination: On the design and evaluation of school programs*. Macmillan.

Emig, J. A. (1971). *The composing processes of twelfth graders*. National Council of Teachers of English.

Encyclopedia Britannica. (1969/2019). *The lottery*. [Video]. YouTube. https://www.youtube.com/watch?v=HZyhVg31iaQ

Ernst, K. (1997). The artists workshop: Widening the reading, writing, and art connections. *Reading & Writing Quarterly:, 13*(4), 355–367.

Esposito, L. (2012). Where to begin? Using place-based writing to connect students with their local communities. *English Journal, 101*(4), 70–76.

Ewald, W. (2001). *I wanna take me a picture: Teaching photography and writing to children*. Beacon Press.

Fahey, K., Lawrence, J., & Paratore, J. (2007). Using electronic portfolios to make learning public. *Journal of Adolescent & Adult Literacy*, 460–471.

Fischer, J. (2006). Killing at close range: A study in intertextuality. *English Journal, 95*(3), 27–31.

Fletcher, R. (1996). *Breathing in, breathing out: Keeping a writer's notebook*. Heinemann.

Flower, L., & Hayes, J. R. (1981). A cognitive process theory of writing. *College Composition and Communication, 32*(4), 365–387.

Francis, P., Reiser, B., & Velasquez, E. (2002). *David gets his drum*. Marshall Cavendish.

Freire, P. (1970/2000). *Pedagogy of the oppressed.* Bloomsbury Academic.

Freire, P., & Macedo, D. (1987). *Literacy: Reading the word and the world.* Routledge.

Gainer, J. S., & Lapp, D. (2010a). *Literacy remix: Bridging adolescents' in and out of school literacies.* International Literacy Association.

Gainer, J. S., & Lapp, D. (2010b). Remixing old and new literacies = Motivated students. *English Journal, 100*(1), 58–64.

Gainer, J. S., Valdez-Gainer, N., & Kinard, T. (2009). The elementary bubble project: Exploring critical media literacy in a fourth-grade classroom. *The Reading Teacher, 62*(8), 674–683.

Gawande, A. (2013, July 29). Slow ideas. *The New Yorker.* https://www.newyorker.com/magazine/2013/07/29/slow-ideas

Gay, G. (2018). *Culturally responsive teaching: Theory, research, and practice* (3rd ed.). Teachers College Press.

Gee, J. P. (1996). *Social linguistics and literacies: Ideology in discourses* (2nd ed.). The Falmer Press.

Gibson, S. (2010). Critical readings: African American girls and urban fiction. *Journal of Adolescent & Adult Literacy, 53*(7), 565–574.

Gilhooly, D., & Lee, E. (2014). The role of digital literacy practices on refugee resettlement: The case of three Karen brothers. *Journal of Adolescent & Adult Literacy, 57*(5), 387–396.

Gilje, Ø., & Groeng, L. M. (2015). The making of a filmmaker: Curating learning identities in early careers. *E-Learning and Digital Media 2015, 12*(2), 212–225.

Gladwell, M. (2002). *The tipping point.* Back Bay Books.

Glasgow, J. (1999). Moon journals: Inquiry into nature, art, literature, and self. *Ohio Reading Teacher, 33*(1), 24–35.

Glover, D., Goransson, L., & Williams, J. L. (2018). This is America [Recorded by Childish Gambino]. Digital download.

Golden, J. (2001). *Reading in the dark: Using film as a tool in the English classroom.* National Council of Teachers of English.

Golden, J. (2006). *Reading in the reel world: Teaching documentaries and other nonfiction texts.* National Council of Teachers of English.

Golding, W. (1954/2003). *Lord of the flies.* Penguin.

Goldstein, D. (2014). *The teacher wars: A history of America's most embattled profession.* Anchor.

Gonzalez, L., Ybarra, M. G., & the Fugitive Literacies Collective. (2020). Multimodal cuentos as fugitive literacies on the Mexico-US borderlands. *English Education, 52*(3), 223–255.

Gonzalez, N., Moll, L. C., & Amanti, C. (2005). *Funds of knowledge: Theorizing practices in households, communities, and classrooms.* Lawrence Erlbaum Associates.

Goodman, S. (2003). *Teaching youth media: A critical guide to literacy, video production, and social change.* Teachers College Press.

Goodman, S. (2018). *It's not about grit: Trauma, inequity, and the power of transformative teaching.* Teachers College Press.

Gorski, K. J. (2020). "My voice matters": High school debaters' acquisition of dominant and adaptive cultural capital. *American Journal of Education, 126*, 293–321.

Graves, D. (1983/2003). *Writing: Teachers and children at work. 20th anniversary edition.* Heinemann.

Graves, D., & Hansen, J. (1983). "The author's chair." *Language Arts, 60*(2), 176–183.

Greene, M. (2001). *Variations on a blue guitar: The Lincoln Center Institute lectures on aesthetic education.* Teachers College Press.

Griffith, J. (2018). Constantly curating: Building text sets and pairings in novel study. *Voices From the Middle, 26*(2), 39–41.

Grimes, N. (2017). *Bronx Masquerade.* Speak.

Gustavson, L. (2008). Influencing pedagogy through the creative practices of youth. In M. L. Hill & L. Vasudevan (Eds.), *Media, learning, and sites of possibility* (pp. 81–114). Peter Lang.

Guthrie, J. T., & Wigfield, A. (1997). Reading engagement: A rationale for theory and teaching. In J. T. Guthrie & A. Wigfield (Eds.), *Reading engagement: Motivating readers through integrated instruction* (pp. 1–12). International Reading Association.

Hadley, J. L. (2019). Engaging the humanity of middle schoolers through community interviews. *Voices From the Middle, 27*(2), 37–39.

Hall, M., & Stahl, K. A. D. (2012). Devillainizing video in support of comprehension and vocabulary instruction. *The Reading Teacher, 65,* 403–406.

Harmon, J. A., & Marquez-Zenkov, K. (2007). Seeing English in the city: Using photography to understand students' literacy relationships. *English Journal, 96*(6), 24–30.

Haymes, S. (1995). *Race, culture, and the city: A pedagogy for Black urban struggle.* State University of New York Press.

Heffernan, L., & Lewison, M. (2009). Keep your eyes on the prize: Critical stance in the middle school classroom. *Voices from the Middle, 17*(2), 19–27.

Heffernan, L., Lewison, M., Bulushi, Z. A., & Park, H. (2020). Breaking news: Kids are fans and critics! Reading with and against the school newsmagazine. *Language Arts, 98*(2), 58–70.

Hendrix, J. (2013, June 5). Winnie-the-Pooh and Penguin take the stage in e-book trial. *Los Angeles Times.* https://www.latimes.com/books/jacketcopy/la-et-jc-winnie-the-pooh-and-penguin-ebook-trial-20130605-story.html

Herrera, S. G. (2016). *Biography-driven culturally responsive teaching* (2nd ed.). Teachers College Press.

HIP HOP CLASSIC. (2010, July 24). *2pac-T.H.U.G.L.I.F.E.(The hate u give little infants fuck everybody)* [Video]. https://www.youtube.com/QCEf557fNYg

Hitchcock, A. (Director). (1960). *Psycho* [Film]. Shamley Productions.

Hodges, A. L. (2010). A critical close-up: Three films and their lessons in critical literacy. *English Journal, 99*(3), 70–75.

Holt, J. (1967/1995). *How children learn* (Revised ed.). Da Capo.

Howell, E. (2017). Expanding argument instruction: Incorporating multimodality and digital tools. *Journal of Adolescent & Adult Literacy, 61,* 533–542.

Huang, S. (2011). Reading "further and beyond the text": Student perspectives of critical literacy in EFL reading and writing. *Journal of Adolescent and Adult Literacy, 55,* 145–154.

Hurst, B. (2005). My journey with learning logs. *Journal of Adolescent & Adult Literacy, 49,* 42–46.

Institute for Student Achievement. (2021). About us. https://www.studentachievement .org/our-story/about-us/

Jackson, S. (1949). The lottery. In *The lottery and other stories*. Farrar, Straus.

Jacobs, H. H. (1989). *Interdisciplinary curriculum: Design and implementation*. Association of Supervision and Curriculum Development.

Jenkins, H. (1992/2013). *Textual poachers: Television fans and participatory culture*. Updated Twentieth Anniversary Edition. Routledge.

Jenkins, H. (2006/2008). *Convergence culture: Where old and new media collide*. New York University Press.

Jenkins, H. (2020). *Comics and stuff*. New York University Press.

Jenkins, P. (Director). (2020). *Wonder Woman 1984* [Film]. Atlas Entertainment.

Jocius, R. (2016). Telling unexpected stories: Students as multimodal artists. *English Journal, 105*(5), 16–22.

Jocius, R. (2020). The CLICK model: Scaffolding multimodal composing for academic purposes. *Language Arts, 97*(3), 146–158.

John-Steiner, V. (1997). *Notebooks of the mind: Explorations of thinking* (Revised ed.). Oxford University Press.

Kahrs, J. (Director). (2012). *Paperman* [Film]. Walt Disney Animation Studios.

Kane, B., & Finger, B. (Creators). (1999–2001). *Batman beyond* [TV series]. Warner Bros. Animation; DC Comics; Warner Bros. Television.

Kelly, L. L. (2019). Building critical classroom community through hip-hop literature. *English Journal, 109*(1), 52–58.

Kinloch, V. (2007). Youth representations of community, art, and struggle in Harlem. *New Directions for Adult and Continuing Education, 116*, 37–49.

Kinloch, V., Burkhard, T., & Penn, C. (2017). When school is not enough: Understanding the lives and literacies of Black youth. *Research in the Teaching of English, 52*(1), 34–54.

Kinney, A. (2012). Loops, lyrics, and literacy: Songwriting as a site of resilience for an urban adolescent. *Journal of Adolescent & Adult Literacy, 55*, 395–404.

Kist, W. (2005). *New literacies in action: Teaching and learning in multiple media*. Teachers College Press.

Kist, W. (2008). Film and video in classroom: Back to the future. In J. Flood, D. Lapp, & S. B. Heath (Eds.), *Handbook of research on teaching literacy through the communicative and visual arts* (Vol. 2, pp. 521–527). Lawrence Erlbaum Associates.

Kist, W. (2010). *The socially networked classroom: Teaching in the new media age*. Corwin.

Kist, W. (2012). Middle schools and new literacies: Looking back and moving forward. *Voices From the Middle, 19*(4), 17–21.

Kist, W. (2013). *The global school: Connecting classrooms and students around the world*. Solution Tree Press.

Kist, W. (2017). Life moments in texts: Analyzing multimodal memoirs of preservice teachers. *English Journal, 106*(3), 63–68.

Kist, W. (2019). Curating your life: Using the writer's notebook that's in your pocket. *Ohio Journal of English Language Arts, 58*(2), 81–83.

Kist, W., Davis, S., & Haynes, G. (2019). *The hate u give*: How one text led to a year-long classroom inquiry project. *Ohio Journal of English Language Arts, 59*(1), 73–77.

Klein, N. (2009). *No logo*. Picador.

Kliebard, H. M. (1986). *The struggle for the American curriculum 1893–1958*. Routledge.

Knobel, M., & Lankshear, C. (2008). Remix: The art and craft of endless hybridization. *Journal of Adolescent & Adult Literacy, 52*(1), 22–33.

Kohn, A. (2006). The trouble with rubrics. *English Journal, 95*(4), 12–15.

Kohn, A. (2010). How to create nonreaders: Reflections on motivation, learning, and sharing power. *English Journal, 100*(1), 16–22.

Kozol, J. (1991/2012). *Savage inequalities: Children in America's schools*. Crown.

Krashen, S. (2013). Access to books and time to read versus the common core state standards and texts. *English Journal, 103*(2), 21–29.

Krueger, E., & Chistel, M. T. (2001). *Seeing and believing: How to teach media literacy in the English classroom*. Heinemann.

Kuhn, T. S. (1962/2012). *The structure of scientific revolutions*. University of Chicago Press.

Ladson-Billings, G. J. (1995). But that's just good teaching! The case for culturally relevant pedagogy. *Theory Into Practice, 34*(3), 159–165. https://doi.org/10.1080/00405849509543675

Ladson-Billings, G. J. (1999). Preparing teachers for diverse student populations: A critical race theory perspective. *Review of Research in Education, 24*, 211–247.

Ladson-Billings, G. J. (2009). *The dreamkeepers: Successful teachers of African American children* (2nd ed.). Jossey-Bass.

Ladson-Billings, G. J. (2014). Culturally relevant pedagogy 2.0: a.k.a. the Remix. *Harvard Educational Review, 84*(1), 74–84.

Lankshear, C., & Knobel, M. (2006). *New literacies: Everyday practices and classroom learning*. Open UP.

Leekeenan, K., & White, H. (2021). Recognition and respect: Centering students' voices through writing groups. *English Journal, 110*(4), 92–99.

Lefferman, J., & Taguchi, E. (Directors). (2019). *After Parkland* [Film]. ABC Documentaries.

Leland, C. H., & Harste, J. C. (1994). Multiple ways of knowing: Curriculum in a new key. *Language Arts, 71*, 337–345.

Lemmons, K. (Director). (2019). *Harriet* [film]. Martin Chase Productions.

Lewis, C. C., Perry, R. R., Friedkin, S., & Roth, J. R. (2012). Improving teaching does improve teachers: Evidence from lesson study. *Journal of Teacher Education, 63*(5) 368–375.

Linklater, R. (Director). (2014). *Boyhood* (Film). IFC Productions; Detour Filmproduction.

Lopez, F. A. (2017). Altering the trajectory of the self-fulfilling prophecy: Asset-based pedagogy and classroom dynamics. *Journal of Teacher Education, 68*(2), 193–212.

Luke, A. (2000). Re/Mediating adolescent literacies. *Journal of Adolescent and Adult Literacy, 43*, 448–461.

Luke, A., & Woods, A. (2009). Critical literacies in schools: A primer. *Voices From the Middle, 17*(2), 9–18.

MacGillivray, L., & Curwen, M. S. (2007). Tagging as a social literacy practice. *Journal of Adolescent and Adult Literacy, 50*, 354–369.

Macrorie, K. (1988). *The I-Search paper*. Heinemann.

Maiers, A. (2012). *Classroom habitudes: Teaching habits and attitudes for 21st century learning*. Solution Tree Press.

Marković, S. (2012). Components of aesthetic experience: Aesthetic fascination, aesthetic appraisal, and aesthetic emotion. *i-Perception, 3*(1), 1–17.

Massimini, F., Csikszentmihalyi, M., & Delle Fave, A. (1988). Flow and biocultural evolution. In M. Csikszentmihalyi & I. S. Csikszentmihalyi (Eds.), *Optimal experience: Psychological studies of flow in consciousness* (pp. 60–81). Cambridge University Press.

Mathieu, P. (2014). A guiding question, some primary research, and dash of rhetorical awareness. In D. Coxwell-Teague & R. F. Lunsford (Eds.), *First-year composition: From theory to practice* (pp. 111–145). Parlor Press.

McCaffrey, M., & Corapi, S. (2017). Creating multicultural and global text sets: A tool to complement the CCSS text exemplars. *Talking Points, 28*(2), 8–17.

McConnel, J. (2019). Fan spaces as third spaces: Tapping into the creative community of fandom. *English Journal, 109*(1), 45–51.

McLaren, P. (1986/1999). *Schooling as a ritual performance* (3rd ed.). Roman & Littlefield.

McLaughlin, M., & Vogt, M. (1996). *Portfolios in teacher education*. International Reading Association.

McLean, C. A. (2010). A space called home: An immigrant adolescent's digital literacy practices. *Journal of Adolescent & Adult Literacy, 54*(1), 13–22

McLean, C. A., & Rowsell, J. (2015). Imagining writing futures: Photography, writing, and technology. *Reading & Writing Quarterly: Overcoming Learning Difficulties, 31*(2), 102–118.

McMillan, S., & Wilhelm, J. (2007). Students' stories: Adolescents constructing multiple literacies through nature journaling. *Journal of Adolescent and Adult Literacy, 50*, 370–377.

Meixner, E., Peel, A., Hendrickson, R., Szczeck, L., & Bousum, K. (2018). Storied lives: Teaching memoir writing through multimodal mentor texts. *Journal of Adolescent & Adult Literacy, 62*, 495–508.

Metz, C. (1974/1991). *Film language: A semiotics of the cinema*. Trans. Michael Taylor. University of Chicago Press.

Michaels, J. R. (2009). Reimagining Coleridge's "Rime of the Ancient Mariner" through visual and performing arts projects. *English Journal, 99*(2), 48–54.

Mihailidis, P. (2015). Digital curation and digital literacy: Evaluating the role of curation in developing critical literacies for participation in digital culture. *E-Learning and Digital Media, 12*(5–6), 443–458. https://doi.org/10.1177/2042753016631868

Mills, K. A., & Unsworth, L. (2017). iPad Animations: Powerful multimodal practices for adolescent literacy and emotional language. *Journal of Adolescent & Adult Literacy, 61*, 609–620.

Moje, E. B. (2008). Youth cultures, literacies, and identities in and out of school. In J. Flood, D. Lapp, & S. B. Heath (Eds.), *Handbook of research on teaching literacy through the communicative and visual arts* (Vol. 2, pp. 207–219). Lawrence Erlbaum Associates.

Monaco, J. (2000). *How to read a film: The world of movies, media, and multimedia* (3rd ed.). Oxford University Press.

Morrell, E., Duenas, R., Garcia, V., & Lopez, J. (2013). *Critical media pedagogy: Teaching for achievement in city schools.* Teachers College Press.

Morrison, T. (1987). *Beloved.* Everyman Press.

Muhammad, G. (2020). *Cultivating genius: An equity framework for culturally and historically responsive literacy.* Scholastic.

Myers, J., & Eberfors, F. (2010). Globalizing English through intercultural critical literacy. *English Education, 42*(2), 148–171.

Nattiv, G. (Director). 2018). *Skin* [Film]. New Native Pictures; Movie Trailer House; Studio Mao.

New London Group. (1996). A pedagogy of multiliteracies: Designing social futures. *Harvard Education Review, 66*(1), 60–92.

Nichols, R. E. (2008). "Kind of like emerging from the shadows": Adolescent girls as multiliteracy pedagogues. In M. L. Hill & L. Vasudevan (Eds.), *Media, learning and sites of possibility* (pp. 119–156). Peter Lang.

Nunez, I. (2019). "Le hacemos la lucha": Learning from Madres Mexicanas' multimodal approaches to raising bilingual, biliterate children. *Language Arts, 97*(1), 7–16.

O'Byrne, I. (2012). *Creating and curating your digital identity.* https://wiobyrne.com/creating-and-curating-your-online-brand/

Ohito, E. O., & the Fugitive Literacies Collective. (2020). "The creative aspect woke me up": Awakening to multimodal essay composition as a fugitive literacy practice. *English Education, 52*(3), 186–222.

Olan, E. L., & Pantano, J. A. (2020). An "Epiphania": Exploring students' identities through multimodal literacies. *English Journal, 109*(4), 78–86.

Oner, D., and Adadan, E. (2011). Use of web-based portfolios as tools for reflection in preservice teacher education. *Journal of Teacher Education, 62*(5), 477–492.

Palincsar, A. S., & Brown, A. L. (1984). Reciprocal teaching of comprehension-fostering and comprehension-monitoring activities. *Cognition and Instruction, 2,* 117–175.

Pantano, J. A. (2020). Dear ELA colleagues and leaders: Here are multimodal learning representations for difficult times and beyond. *English Leadership Quarterly, 43*(1), 11–14.

Peele, J. (Director). (2017). *Get out* [Film]. Blumhouse Productions.

Perrin, A. (2021, June 3). *Mobile technology and home broadband 2021.* Pew Research Center. https://www.pewresearch.org/internet/2021/06/03/mobile-technology-and-home-broadband-2021/

Phillips, T. (Director and producer) (2019). *Joker.* [Motion picture]. Warner Brothers.

Plair, D. (Director). (2019). *First day back* [Motion picture]. Flower Ave. Films.

Player, G. D. (2021). "My color of my name": Composing critical self-celebration with girls Of color through a feminist of color writing pedagogy. *Research in the Teaching of English, 55,* 216–240.

Pleasants, H. M. (2008). Negotiating identity projects: Exploring the digital storytelling experiences of three African American girls. In M. L. Hill & L. Vasudevan (Eds.), *Media, learning, and sites of possibility* (pp. 205–233). Peter Lang.

Polacco, P. (2012). *The art of Miss Chew.* G. P. Putnam's Sons Books for Young Readers.

Postman, N., & Weingartner, C. (1971). *Teaching as a subversive activity*. Delta.

Potter, J. (2012). *Digital media and learner identity: The new curatorship*. Palgrave Macmillan.

Potter, J., & Gilje, Ø. (2015). Curation as a new literacy practice. *E-learning and Digital Media, 12*(2), 123–127. https://doi.org/10.1177/2042753014568150

Poveda, D. (2012). Literacy artifacts and the semiotic landscape of a Spanish secondary school. *Reading Research Quarterly, 47*(1), 61–88.

Purves, A. C., Rogers, T., & Soter, A. O. (1990). *How porcupines make love: Teaching a response-centered literature curriculum*. National Council of Teachers of English.

Ranker, J., & Mills, K. (2014). New directions for digital video creation in the classroom. *Journal of Adolescent & Adult Literacy, 57*(6), 440–443.

Raschka, C. (1997). *Charlie Parker played be bop*. Scholastic.

Resnick, D. P. (1991). Historical perspectives on literacy and schooling. In S. R. Graubard (Ed.), *Literacy: An overview by fourteen experts* (pp. 15–32). Hill and Wang.

Reynolds, J., & Kiely, B. (2017). *All American boys*. Atheneum.

Rhoades, M. (2020). A contemporary arts-based approach to critical multimodal literacy. *Language Arts, 97*, 178–185.

Rice, Mary. (2007). Using customer reviews to build reading skills. *English Journal, 97*:1, 89–93.

Rish, R., & Caton, R. (2011). Building fantasy worlds together with collaborative writing: Creative, social, and pedagogic challenges. *English Journal, 100*(5), 21–28.

Rivera, N. K. (2020). Chicanx murals: Decolonizing place and (re)writing the terms of composition. *College Communication and Composition, 72*(1), 118–149.

Robinson, B. (2018). Lights, camera, courage: Authentic assessment and multimodal composition. *English Journal, 108*(1), 25–31.

Rodesiler, L. (2019). Stick to sports: Leveraging sports culture to promote critical literacy. *Language Arts, 96*(5), 335–338.

Rogers, R. (2002). "That's what you're here for, you're suppose to tell us": Teaching and learning critical literacy. *Journal of Adolescent & Adult Literacy, 45*, 772–787.

Romano, T. (2000). *Blending genre, altering style: Writing multigenre papers*. Heinemann.

Roozen, K. (2009). "Fan fic-ing" English studies: A case study exploring the interplay of vernacular literacies and disciplinary engagement. *Research in the Teaching of English, 44*(2), 136–169.

Rosenblatt, L. M. (1938/1995). *Literature as exploration* (5th ed.). Modern Language Association.

Rosenblatt, L. M. (1978). *The reader, the text, the poem: The transactional theory of the literary work*. Southern Illinois University Press.

Ross, A. (2010). *Listen to this*. Farrar, Straus and Giroux.

Rousseau, J.-J. (1762/1979). *Émile: Or on education*. Basic Books.

Rozansky, C. L., & Aagesen, C. (2010). Low-achieving readers, high expectations: Image theatre encourages critical literacy. *Journal of Adolescent & Adult Literacy, 53*(6), 458–466. https://doi.org/10.1598/JAAL.53.6.2

Ruggieri, C. (2002). Multigenre, multiple intelligences, and transcendentalism. *English Journal, 92*(2), 60–68.

Rust, J., & Ballard, S. (2016). I am/you see: Traversing literacies from page to screen to body. *English Journal, 105*(5), 61–67.

Rydell, M. (Director). (1981). *On Golden Pond* [Moving picture]. IPC Films; Incorporated Television Company (ITC).

Schmertz, J. (2016). Textual intervention and film literacy. *English Journal, 105*(5), 48–52.

Schofield, A., & Rogers, T. (2004). At play in fields of ideas. *Journal of Adolescent & Adult Literacy, 48*, 238–248.

Schön, D. A. (1983). *The reflective practitioner: How professionals think in action.* New York: Basic Books.

Semali, L. M., & Pailliotet, A. W. (Eds.). (1999). *Intermediality: The teachers' handbook of critical media literacy* (1st ed.). Routledge.

Shakur, T. (2009). *The rose that grew from concrete.* MTV Books.

Sharma, S., & Deschaine, M. (2015). The five Cs of digital curation: Supporting twenty-first-century teaching and learning. *InSight: A Journal of Scholarly Teaching, 10*, 19–24.

Silberman, M. (1996). *Active learning: 101 strategies to teach any subject.* Allyn & Bacon.

Simon, R. (2012). "Without comic books, there would be no me": Teachers as connoisseurs of adolescents' literate lives. *Journal of Adolescent and Adult Literacy, 55*, 516–526.

Simos, E. (2015, August). Genius hour: Critical inquiry and differentiation. *English Leadership Quarterly*, 2–4.

Skinner, E. (2007). Writing workshop meets critical media literacy: Using magazines and movies as mentor texts. *Voices From the Middle, 15*(2), 30–39.

Smith, B. E. (2017). Composing across modes: A comparative analysis of adolescents' multimodal composing processes. *Learning, Media and Technology, 42*(3), 259–278.

Smith, B. E. (2019). Mediational modalities: Adolescents collaboratively interpreting literature through digital multimodal composing. *Research in the Teaching of English, 53*, 197–222.

Smith, P. (2018, October 8). Does Nikolas Smith deserve to die? *New York Times Upfront Magazine.* https://www.kingstoncityschools.org/cms/lib/NY24000343/Centricity/Domain/271/Does%20Nikolas%20Cruz%20Deserve%20to%20Die%20Oct%208.pdf

Spiegelman, A. (1986). *Maus : A survivor's tale.* Pantheon Books

Spielberg, S. (Director). (2018). *Ready Player One* [Moving picture]. Warner Bros.

Spottiswoode, R. (1950/2011). *A grammar of the film: An analysis of film technique.* Read Books.

Srsen, K., & Kist, W. (2015). "I wanted to film, so I read the book": Filmmaking in the English classroom. In T. Rasinski, K. Pytash, & R. Ferdig (Eds.), *Using technology to enhance reading: Innovative approaches to literacy instruction* (pp. 175–186). Solution Tree Press.

Stanton, C. R., & Sutton, K. (2012). "I guess I do know a good story": Re-envisioning writing process with Native American students and communities. *English Journal, 102*(2), 78–84.

Staples, J. M. (2008). "Do you remember": Confronting post-9/11 censorship through critical questioning and poetic devices. *English Journal, 97*(5), 81–87.

Street, B. V. (1995). *Social literacies: Critical approaches to literacy in development, ethnography and education.* Longman.

Street, B. V. (2012). Society reschooling. *Reading Research Quarterly, 47,* 216–227.

Taba, H. (1967). *Teacher's handbook for elementary social studies.* Addison-Wesley.

Tan, L., & Guo, L. (2010). From print to critical multimedia literacy: One teacher's foray into new literacies practices. *Journal of Adolescent & Adult Literacy, 53,* 315–324.

Thomas, A. (2017). *The hate u give.* Balzer + Bray.

Thomas, A. (2007). Blurring and breaking through the boundaries of narrative, literacy, and identity in adolescent fan fiction. In M. Knobel, & C. Lankshear (Eds.), *A new literacies sampler* (pp. 137–165). Peter Lang.

Thompson, M. (2008). Multimodal teaching and learning: Creating spaces for content teachers. *Journal of Adolescent and Adult Literacy, 52,* 144–153.

Thompson, G., & Rath, R. (n.d.). *The Jackson sit-in.* https://www.sps186.org /downloads/basic/664407/jacksonsitin.pdf

Time to assert American values. (1994, April 13). *The New York Times.* https://www .nytimes.com/1994/04/13/opinion/time-to-assert-american-values.html

Toliver, S. R. (2017). Unlocking the cage: Empowering literacy representations in Netflix's *Luke Cage* series. *Journal of Adolescent & Adult Literacy, 61,* 621–630.

Trier, J. (2006). Reconceptualizing literacy through a discourses perspective by analyzing literacy events represented in films about schools. *Journal of Adolescent & Adult Literacy, 49,* 510–523.

Tsybulsky, D. (2020). Digital curation for promoting personalized learning: A study of secondary-school science students' learning experiences. *Journal of Research on Technology in Education, 52*(3), 429–440. https://doi.org/10.1080 /15391523.2020.1728447

Turner, J. D., & Bailey, A. R. (2020). Beyond "Broken Tests": Supporting powerful reading for urban boys through the brilliant boys' book club. *Language Arts, 97*(6), 376–383.

Vacca, R. T., Vacca, J. L., & Mraz, M. (2020). Content area reading: Literacy and learning across the curriculum. 13th edition. Pearson.

van der Veen, J. (2012). Draw your physics homework? Art as a path to understanding in physics teaching. *American Educational Research Journal, 49,* 356–407.

van Leeuwen, T. (2018). Aesthetics and text in the digital age. In K. A. Mills, A. Stornaiuolo, A. Smith, & J. Z. Pandya (Eds.), *Handbook of writing, literacies, and education in digital cultures* (pp. 285–300). Routledge.

Van Manen, M. (1977). Linking ways of knowing with ways of being practical. *Curriculum Inquiry, 6*(3), 205–228.

Varnon, D. (1997). Enriching remedial programs with the arts. *Reading & Writing Quarterly: Overcoming Learning Difficulties, 13*(4), 325–331.

Verlaan, W. (2017). Through the mind's eye: Using multimodal assignments to build engagement and comprehension. *Journal of Adolescent & Adult Literacy, 61,* 453–456.

Walsh-Moorman, E. (in press). Bringing in other voices through digital source curation. In M. Christel & W. Kist (Eds.), *Bringing critical media literacy into ELA classrooms.* National Council of Teachers of English.

Wasser, J. D., & Bresler, L. (1996). Working in the interpretive zone: Conceptualizing collaboration in qualitative research terms. *Educational Researcher, 25*(5), 5–15.

What is school for? (2019, April 8). [Video]. YouTube. https://www.youtube.com/watch?v=07mK-Wb2WJQ

White, B., & Lemieux, A. (Eds.). (2017). *Mapping holistic learning: An introductory guide to aesthetigrams*. Peter Lang.

Williamson, L. (2009). Virtual seating in the Globe theatre: Appreciating film adaptations of Shakespeare's plays. *English Journal, 99*(1), 71–73.

Wills, J. (2021). *Thinking protocols for learning*. Solution Tree Press.

Wissman, K. K. (2008). "This is what I see": (Re)envisioning photography as a social practice. In M. L. Hill & L. Vasudevan (Eds.), *Media, learning, and sites of possibility* (pp. 13–45). Peter Lang.

Woo, Y. Y. J. (2008). Engaging new audiences: Translating research into popular media. *Educational Researcher, 37*(6), 321–329.

Worlds, M., & Miller, H. C. (2019). Miles Morales: Spider-Man and reimagining the canon for racial justice. *English Journal, 108*(4), 43–50.

Young, C., & Rasinski, T. (2013). Student-produced movies as a medium for literacy development. *The Reading Teacher, 66*(8), 670–675. https://doi.org/10.1002/TRTR.1175

Yousafzai, M., & Lamb, C. (2013). *I am Malala*. Back Bay Books.

Zenkov, K., Harmon, J., Bell, A., Ewaida, M., & Lynch, M. R. (2011). Seeing our city, students, and school: Using photography to engage diverse youth with our English classes. *English Education, 43*, 369–389.

Index

About the Author

William Kist, PhD, is professor emeritus of education at Kent State University. Bill has been working with schools and educators on national and international levels for 20 years, focusing on the areas of integrating technology, teaching online, and using high-yield instructional strategies, particularly in urban settings. A sought-out speaker, Bill has presented for both education associations and entertainment conventions such as the Denver Comic-Con and the Pop Culture Association. An author of over 50 articles, _Curating a Literacy Life_ is Bill's fifth book. He can be found online at williamkist.com and on Twitter: @williamkist.